ספר בנסוע
SEFER BINSOA

© Marc Michaels

ISBN 978-0-9810947-7-9

5771/2010

**Fifth Edition
Revised and Expanded**
5777/2017

The cover image for this book sent to me by my scribal teacher
Vivian Solomon *z'l* from a section of *Torah* I saw
framed in the study of famous British *sofer* Chaim Samson.
It has the two *nuns* written as part of the text
and not written separately bracketing the verses.

ספר בנסוע

SEFER BINSOA

**For Avielah Barclay
my loving wife**

Published by Kulmus Publishing through lulu.com

ISBN 978-0-9810947-7-9
Copyright © Marc Michaels 5771/2010
Fifth Edition 5777/2017

The moral right of the author has been asserted.
No part of this publication may be reproduced, stored in a retrieval system or transmitted in any form or by any means, electronic, mechanical, photocopying, recording, scanning or otherwise except under the terms of the Copyright, Designs and Patents Act 1998.

Cover illustration and design © Marc Michaels 5771/2010
Typeset in Times New Roman and Frank Ruhl.

Above: an illustration based on the two verses and the reversed nunim *drawn by the author long before training as a* Sofer *(scribe).*
Even before becoming a scribe, these special marks in the Torah *fascinated me and so I was collecting commentaries and opinions on them for years - many of which have found their way into this book.*

CONTENTS

Bamidbar 10:35-36	5
Introduction	6
So what's the point?	28
In a relationship with ... God	36
Protect and Survive	51
Mission Possible	58
The 3Rs	70
Conclusion	78
Bibliography	80

There are many images in this book that
contain the Holy Name of God.
Please take care to ensure that these
do not become torn or erased or thrown away.

Conventions:
In order to maintain a consistent approach the following conventions have been employed: a) English translations of Hebrew text are generally given in brackets ( ), and try to adhere as far as possible to the literal meaning of the words, to convey the economy of the language. Where this would render the translation difficult to understand, linking phrases or explanations are supplied in square brackets [ ], b) Hebrew words or phrases translated once are generally not translated again when they occur, c) Hebrew words that are not quotations are generally given in transliteration, e.g. *Midrash*, *Tanna*, Transliterations are consistent through the body of the book, but may differ from transliterations as they appear in quotations from secondary sources in spelling or capitalisation. Similarly, transliterated Hebrew words are shown in italics in the body of the book, but may not be in a quotation from a secondary source where italics were not employed, d) The Hebrew names for the Biblical or Rabbinical texts are generally used rather than any Latin equivalents, i.e. *D'varim* rather than Deuteronomy,unless in quotation from a secondary source or the better known Latinised name e.g. Moses, Joshua.

BAMIDBAR 10:35-36

Picture from my copy of the Mikra'ot G'dolot, Pardes *1951.*

נ ‎ לה‎ וַיְהִי בִּנְסֹעַ הָאָרֹן וַיֹּאמֶר מֹשֶׁה קוּמָה | יְהֹוָה וְיָפֻצוּ אֹיְבֶיךָ וְיָנֻסוּ מְשַׂנְאֶיךָ מִפָּנֶיךָ: לו וּבְנֻחֹה יֹאמַר שׁוּבָה יְהֹוָה רִבְבוֹת אַלְפֵי יִשְׂרָאֵל: נ פ

³⁵ And it was with the going forward of the ark [that] Moses would say [*lit.* said] 'Arise Lord and your enemies will be scattered and those that hate you you will flee before you ...

³⁶ ... and when it rested, he said [*lit.* will say] 'Return Lord, [to] the myriads of the thousands [of the tents/troops/families] of Israel.'

INTRODUCTION

Aside from their familiar use in the service at the opening and closing of the ark, these two *p'sukim* (verses) from the *sedra* בהעלתך *b'ha'alot'cha* (lit. in your going up) are unique[1] for, in the majority of *Torah* scrolls and biblical manuscripts, *Bamidbar* 10:35-36 is encased between two critical marks, each taking the form of an inverted *nun* and called in Hebrew נון מנוזרת *nun m'nuzeret* (isolated *nun*) or נון הפוכה *nun hafucha* (inverted *nun*), almost as if they are in some sort of parenthesis.

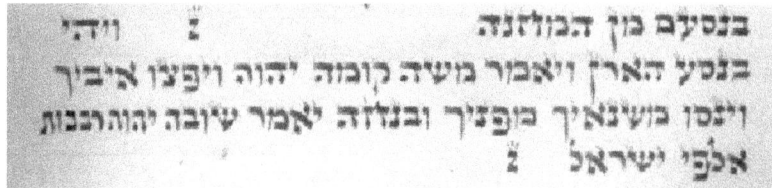

Above: an excerpt from a Sefer Torah *showing the* nun hafuchot *around the two verses.*

Indeed, Tov explains that this is exactly what they are. He notes that 'actually these signs are misunderstood scribal signs

---

1. Historically there is another example of an upside down *nun* in *Torah* - a *nun sofit* (final letter) that occurs in וימת תרח בחרן (and Terach died in Charan (*B'reshit* 11:32)), however this is no longer in use and such a scroll would most likely be declared *pasul* (invalid) by most authorities. In some *Sifrey Torah* it is written with a sloping *gag* (roof).

 *Torah Sh'lemah* vol. 29 page shows some example forms that have been seen (left).

for the removal of inappropriate segments, viz. the Greek letters ... *antisigma* ... and *sigma*'. He further explains that these 'para-textual elements... were not meant to be copied into the subsequent copying. Rather, the sections indicated with the inverted *nunim* ... were meant to be removed. However they were maintained perpetually in the [Massoretic] tradition.'[1]

Leiman, notes that 'the precise form and position of the inverted *nuns* varies in the scroll and manuscripts.'[2] For example Solomon Luria,[3] writing in the late 18th century found twelve different arrangements, though there are apparently considerably more and much confusion in the commentaries as to what they should look like. *Torah Sh'lemah* vol. 29 also gives several versions from *Sifrey Torah* that the author Rabbi M. Kasher had seen.[4] *Mishnat Avraham*[5] too brings several different possible forms. *Minchat Shai*[6] also records the debate over variants.

---

1. Tov, E, *Textual Criticism of the Hebrew Bible, 3rd Ed.*, Fortress Press, 2012, p51. Indeed we will later see where the rabbis believed these verses should have been repositioned.
2. Leiman S, *Journal of Biblical Literature*, Sept. 1979, p346/7.
3. Solomon Luria (1510-1573) Ashkenazi *posek* (decider of Jewish law) is also referred to as Maharshal. Known for his halachic work *Yam Shel Sh'lomo*, and his Talmudic commentary *Chochmat Sh'lomo*.
4. *Torah Sh'lemah* Vol. 29, American Bible Encyclopedia Society Inc., Jerusalem 1978. This is a part of the huge multi-volumed work being a 'talmudic-midrashic encyclopedia of the Pentateuch'. This volume contains a very unique collection of what I term visual *midrash* with examples of special letters found throughout many scrolls that Rabbi Kasher studied . He describes these scribal oddities and brings the opinions of many sources and commentators on their history and form.
5. *Mishnat Avraham* is a collection of *halachot* and responsa collated by Avraham b. Zvi Yaffo and draws on the work of the *L'vush* (Mordechai Yaffo) and was written in 1830.
6. Written by Y'didyah Sh'lomo ben Abraham Norzi (Mantua 1560-1626) who consulted many manuscripts publishing the work as *Goder Perez*. It became *Minchat Shai* when published by Raphael Chayyim Basila, who added to it some notes and appended a list of 900 variations (Mantua 1742-44).

Above: Torah Sh'lemah *variants. Below: excerpt from* Minchat Shai.

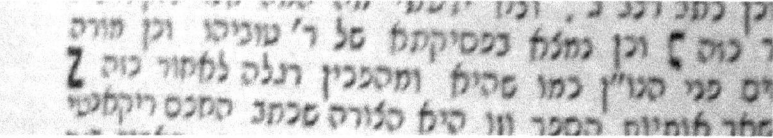

Whichever source one looks at there is universal agreement that no-one knows exactly what the forms of the *nun* should be and that there is much variance between congregational scrolls and also in the personal *Sifrey Torah* of very famous and worthy men who would be very *machmir* (strict) to ensure that they were following the 'right' opinion.

Above: The section from Keset Hasofer *(The Inkwell of the Scribe) a core halachic text for* sofrut *(scribal practice) by Sh'lomo Ganzfried,[1] which discusses the forms of the* nun hafucha. *See translation on p15-16.*

---

1. *Keset Hasofer* was written by Sh'lomo Ganzfried (1804-1886) in Ungvar, Hungary in 1835 and it was his first published work. Ganzfried however, is best known for his later work the *Kitsur Shulchan Aruch*, a summary of the *halachah* needed for daily living. *Keset Hasofer* being a similar work though summarising the rules for scribes, is an excellent source laying out the *halacha l'ma'aseh* (lit. laws for doing).

Thus there seems to be no 'right' opinion.

A page from Mishnat Avraham *chapter 24 - Sha'ar Ha-Nun (the gate of the* nun) *detailing many options that he has seen. These are shown in both the core text and the surrounding commentary.*

Variant forms can also be seen in the early codices that served as the *tikkunim* (copyist's guides) for scribes and master record for the *Massorah* (agreed text).[1]

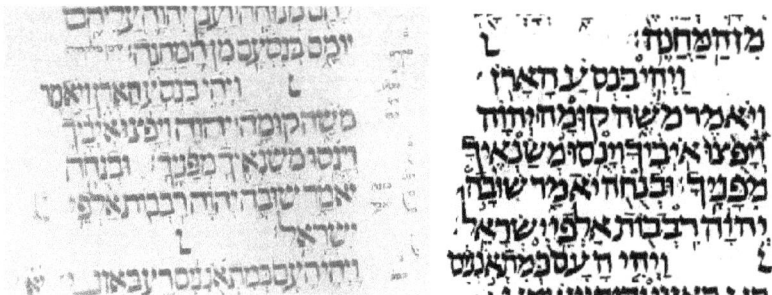

Above right: From the oldest extant manuscript, the Leningrad Codex B19A.[2] Above left: The section as it appears in the Lisbon manuscript.[3]

Below: The section as it appears in an early Spanish manuscript known as the Codex Hillely.[4]

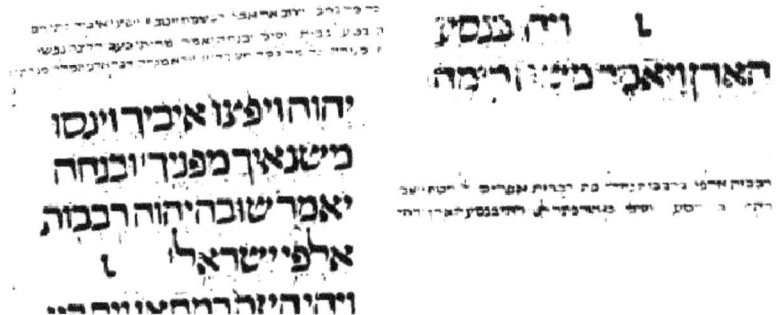

And, in my many years of fixing *Sifrey*, as a *Sofer STa"M*, I have also been fortunate enough to see many variants too.

---

1. The *Massorah* is the authoritative Hebrew text of the *Tanach*. It defines the precise letter-text of the biblical books in Judaism, as well as their vocalization and accentuation.
2. Written in 1008 or 1009. Image: Wikimedia commons.
3. The Lisbon Bible is arguably the most accomplished dated codex. Samuel ben Samuel Ibn Musa completed the work in 1482. British Library Or. MS 2626. © The British Library Board (Or. MS 2626).
4. Codex Hillely is a manuscript of the *Torah* from the year 1241, from Toledo, Spain. It is kept in the Jewish Theological Seminary library in New York.

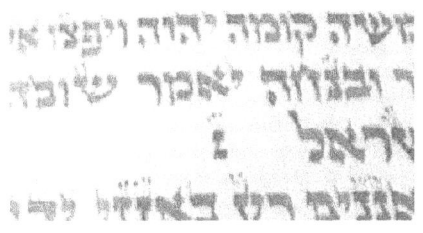
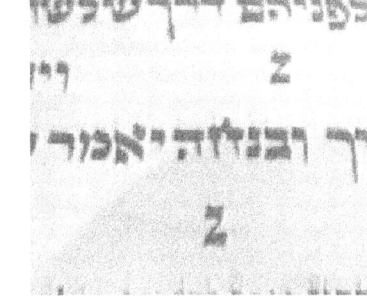

Some variant forms from Sifrey Torah *I have checked.*

Above left: a fairly standard reversed nun. *Above right: a kind of 'Z' shaped form without* taggin *(decorative strokes). Below left:* taggin *on the bottom of the letter form with quite an elongated roof. Below right: a damaged section but showing the 'Z' shape with* taggin.

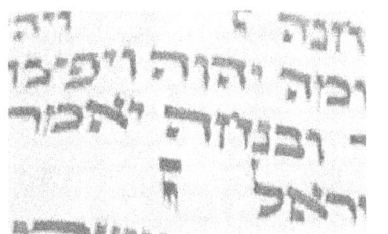
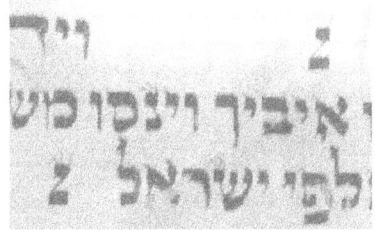

Below left: The 'z' shape but the first one is reversed looking like a squared 's'. Below right: a reversed nun *with a very long base and no* taggin.

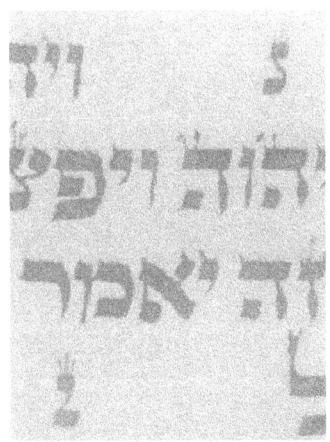
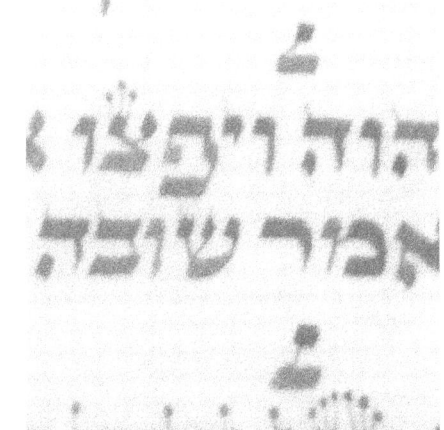

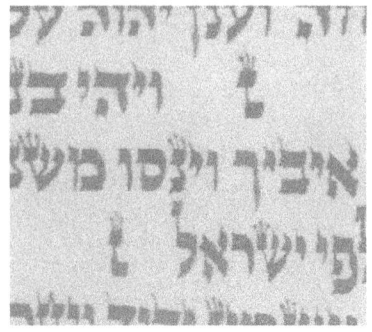 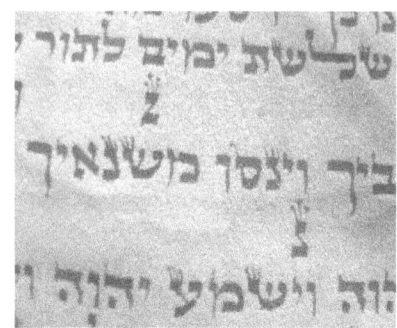

Above left: This time the top of the reversed nun *slopes backwards. Above right: The 'Z' and the 'S' but this time with the 'S' shape at the start and the 'Z' at the end.*

Below: a very pronounced gag *(roof) on the reversed letter matching the normal* nun *for this* sofer *(scribe).*

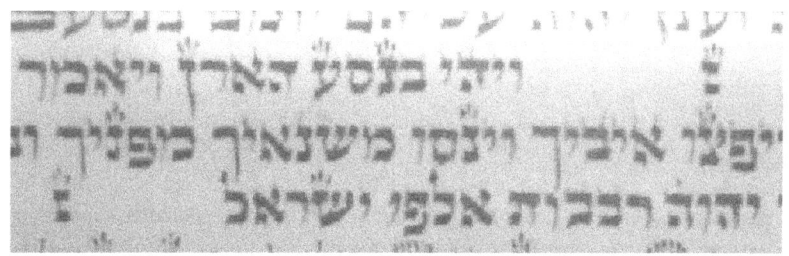

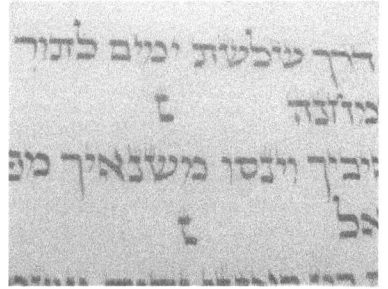 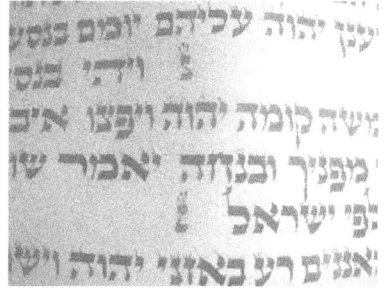

Above left: again a very pronounced roof and base on a quite thin and delicate letter forms. Above right: The 'S' shape followed by a more traditional reversed letter nun.

Leitner, too, notes that 'there are differing opinions as to the way these two letters should be written ... one opinion states that these two inverted letters are actually written upside down, with the wide side at the top. Another opinion maintains these letters are inverted from back to front but are not written upside down.' He further explains that 'the Recanti inverts the letter *nuns* in a different way. He explains that the top part of the letter should be written in the normal format facing towards the left. The inversion takes place, half way down the leg of the letter, thereby forming a "Z" shape, symbolising a person kneeling down in prayer, as they did in the *Beis haMikdash*.'[1]

It should also be noted that the appearance of an upside down *nun* is not unique to the *Torah*[2] as there are no less than seven of them appearing in *T'hillim* 107. There is relatively little comment on those *nuns* and their exact form. The picture below shows how they appear in the famous Allepo Codex[3] and after that how they appear in the *k'laf* of *T'hillim* that is located in the synagogue area to the side of the *Kotel* (Western Wall) that I saw and photographed on a visit there.

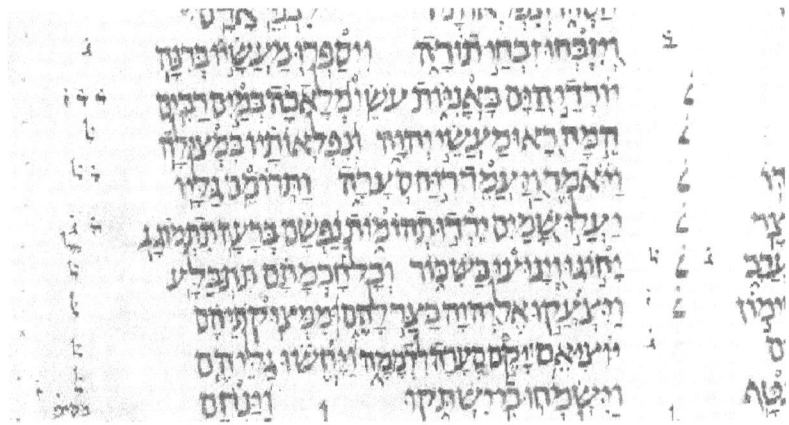

---

1. Leitner, D, *Understanding the Alef-Beis*, Feldheim, Jerusalem, 2007, p284.
2. Over and above the upside down *nun sofit* referenced on page 6.
3. The Aleppo Codex is a bound manuscript considered to be the most authoritative version of the Massoretic text, written c. 930. Unfortunately the section containing *Bamidbar* 10:35-36 is not extant.

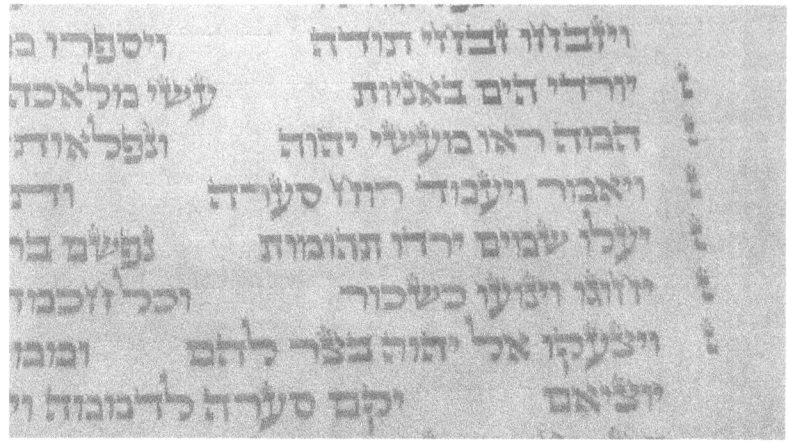

Indeed, the form of an upside down *nun* (though clearly not supposed to be one) can be also be seen in other codices, where it is used a space filler to ensure that a column is fully justified. It is possible that over time, it is this usage that has cemented the idea of this particular form for this special sign.

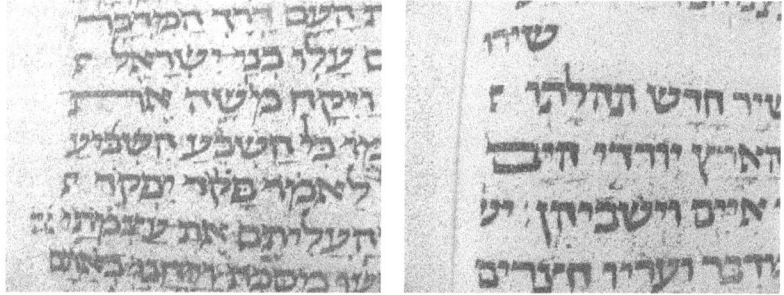

Above: two examples where a form similar to an upside down nun is used to fill in space at the end of a line from manuscripts held on the Bodlian Library Oxford. Left: From the sedra *B'shalach. Right: a section from* T'hillim.

Returning to the *nunim hafuchot* around *Bamidbar* 10:35-36, *Keset Hasofer* (16:7-8) explains in detail:

ז: בפסקא של ויהי בנסוע הארון צריכין לעשות שתי נונין מנוזרות ונחלקו הפוסקים בעניינים והעיקר הוא להלכה ולמעשה שיש לעשותן בריוח שבין הפרשיות ואי משום שממעטין בשיעור ריוח הפרשה יש להניח אחרי כלות מן המחנה שהיא לפני ויהי בנסוע באמצע השיטה ריוח כדי ט' אותיות ואח"כ הנון המנוזרת ואח"כ שוב ריוח ב' או ג' אותיות ואח"כ יתחיל ויהי בנסוע באותה שיטה כדין סתומה ואחר כלות אלפי ישראל יניח ג"כ ריוח כמו ב' או ג' אותיות ואח"כ נו"ן מנוזרת ואח"כ ריוח ט' אותיות באותה שיטה ובראש השיטה השני יתחיל פרשת ויהי העם וגו' ובזה יוצא מידי כל החששות (נוב"ק סי' ע"ד וכ"כ בבנ"י ובמנחת שי דלא כמ"ש מהרש"ל להפוך הנו"ן של בנסוע והנו"ן של כמתאננים)

ח: צורת הנונין האלו יש שמניחין הנו"ן כמות שהיא רק שמהפכים רגלה לאחור כזה ויש שמהפכין כל הנו"ן לאחור כזה (שתי הצורית הביא באור תורה והוא הסכים לצורת השני אבל בבני"ו הסכים לצורת הראשונה) ואם לא עשה כלל הני נוני"ן יש להכשיר את הס"ת בדיעבד (תשו' מהרי"ס לובלין ובנ"יו דלא כהמרש"ל) (ע' חקירה י"ז)

(7: In the section of 'and it was when the Ark moved' one must make two reversed *nuns* and the authorities are divided over the matter of them. And the root of the issue for [both] the law [i.e. theory] and the deed [i.e. practice], is that one should make them in the gap between the sections, and so that one does not lessen the measure of the space of the section, one must leave after finishing [the words] 'from the camp' (*Bamidbar* 10:34) that is before 'and it was when the Ark moved' (*Bamidbar* 10:35) in the middle of the line a gap in order [to fit] nine letters. And after that the reversed *nun*. And after that another gap of two or three letters and after that he will start 'and it was when the Ark moved' on that same line like the rule for the closed section. And, after completing 'the thousands of Israel' (*Bamidbar* 10:35) he leaves also a gap of two to three letters. And after that a reversed *nun* and after that a gap of nine letters on the same line and at the head of the second line he begins 'and it was when the people etc ...' (*Bamidbar* 10:36). And by this he will satisfy all the suggestions[1] [as to how it might be] (*Noda b'Y'huda Kamma*[2] 74, and similarly in the *B'ney Yonah*[3] and in *Minchat Shai* [and] not as the Maharshal says to make upside down the *nun* of *binsoa* [going forward] and the *nun* of *k'mit'onanim* [as murmerers].

8: The forms of the *nuns* are these. There are those who leave the *nun* as it is normally only that they turn its leg backwards like this [Ganzfried includes an image here][4] and there are those who reverse the whole *nun* like this [again an image is included here] (the two forms are brought in the *Or Torah*[5] and he agrees to the second form but in the *B'ney Yonah* he agrees to the first form) and if one did not include the *nuns*, there are those who validate the *Torah* after the event. (Responsa of the Maharam of Lublin[6] and *B'ney Yonah* and not as the Maharshal (c.f. example 17.))

As Ganzfried mentions - and indeed disagrees with - the *nuns* of the *vayehi binsoa* section have not always been separate to the actual text, but were part of the actual words, as the scan of a 700 year old scroll below shows.[7] This was the first time I had seen this tradition, but I have seen and recorded several examples since.

---

1. *Lit.* hunches.
2. Written by Yechezkel ben Yehuda Landau (1713-1793).
3. Written by Yonah Landsofer of Bohemia. (1678-1712).
4. See page 8.
5. Written by Menachem de Lonzano (d.1608).
6. Meir ben Gedalia (1558-1616) best known for his commentary on the *Talmud*, *Me'ir Einai Chachamim*.
7. The cover image for this book sent to me by my scribal teacher Vivian Solomon *z'l* from a section of *Torah* I first saw framed in the study of famous British *sofer* Chaim Samson.

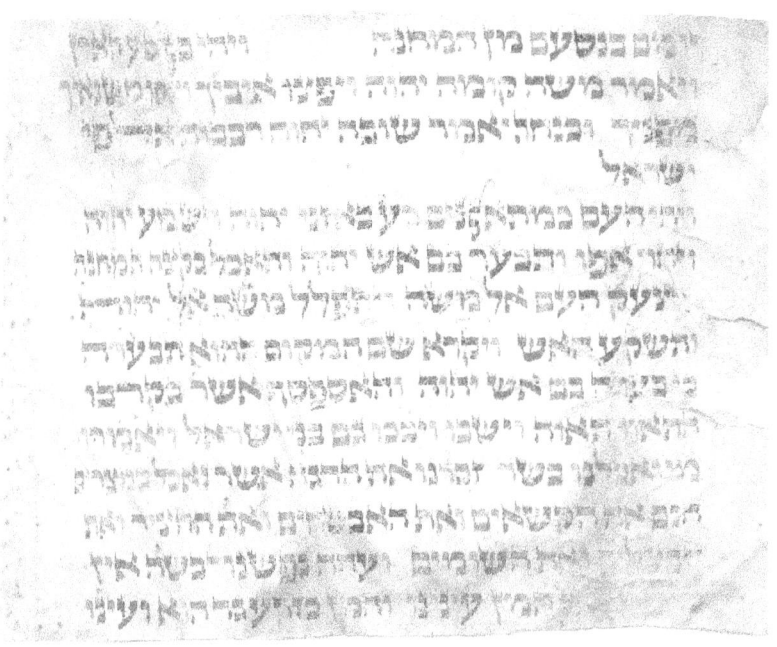

The *nuns* themselves in this instance are decorated with *taggin* and swirls above and below in a kabbalistic style as found in examples brought in *Torah Sh'lemah* Vol. 29.

The first *nun* is in בנסע *binsoa* (when it travelled) and is backwards whilst the second is in the word כמתאננים *k'miton'nim* (as murmerers) in the *pasuk* (verse) following our section - i.e. 10:37. Leitner notes that 'the Rokeach [similarly] ... is of the opinion that in the second word in that passage ויהי בנסע the נ is written backwards, with the leg of the letter pointing towards the right-hand side, and no inverted letters surround this passage.'[1]

---

1. Leitner, *op. cit.*, p284.

One *Torah* that I have almost rewritten during its extensive repair is known as the Alexander *Torah*. This Torah features in no less than two books (and now a third) - the bestseller *Hans and Rudolph - German Jew and the Hunt for the Kommandant of Aushwitz* by Thomas Harding and also *Three Rabbis in a Vicarage* by Antony Godfrey. The *Torah* itself has had a fairly chequered past and it is no small miracle that it survived at all to even reach my workspace for restoration.

It was commissioned in 1790 by Moses Alexander (1814-1881, the great-great-great grandfather of Hanns Alexander, the hero of the aforementioned book) in Thalmässing, a small town near Nuremberg in Germany. It is packed full of fascinating and at times rare kabbalistic features and indeed it too featured the reversed *nuns* within the body of the text on בנסע and כמתאננים.

Similar is found in this Sefardi Torah below.

Also below in this Ashkenazi script Torah written in the 17th Century, Add MS 11828.[1]

וַיְהִי בִּנְסֹעַ וְעָנָן יְהוָה עֲלֵיהֶם יוֹמָם בְּנָסְעָם מִן
הָ וַיְהִי בִּנְסֹעַ הָאָרֹן וַיֹּאמֶר מֹשֶׁה
יְהוָה וְיָפֻצוּ אֹיְבֶיךָ וְיָנֻסוּ מְשַׂנְאֶיךָ מִפָּנֶיךָ

וַיְהִי הָעָם כְּמִתְאֹנְנִים רַע בְּאָזְנֵי יְהוָה וַיִּשְׁמַע
יְהוָה וַיִּחַר אַפּוֹ וַתִּבְעַר בָּם אֵשׁ יְהוָה וַתֹּאכַל בִּקְצֵה

This custom is further reinforced by some *tikkunim* too, as seen in the Venice *Tikkun* below.[2]

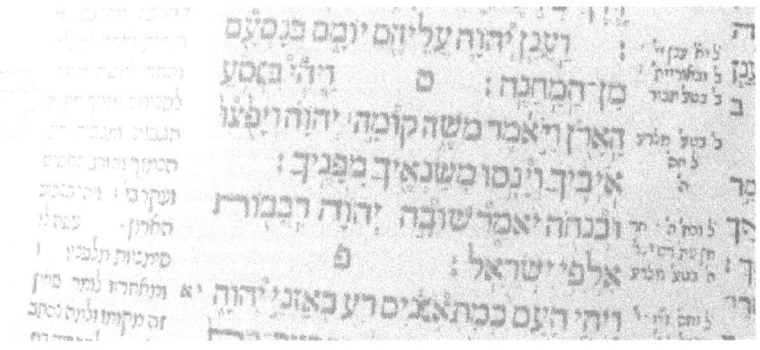

Ginsburg however suggests that this was the result of 'the later Massorites *(sic)*' and that it is a 'striking illustration of the anxiety to obliterate all the early traces of critical signs as to the condition of the text ... in accordance with nearly all the best Codices, some MSS. exhibit the inverted Nun in a word in the text itself.'[3]

---

1. © The British Library Board (Add MS 11828).
2. Published by Daniel Bomberg, ed. Jacob ben Hayyim ibn Adonijah in Venice 1524.
3. Ginsburg, C D, *Introduction to the Massoretico-Critical Edition of the Hebrew Bible*, Trinitarian Bible Society, London 1897, p345.

There is indeed additional debate, and some opinions were that the second *nun* was actually in the word ובנחה *u'v'nucha* (and when it rested) such as is seen in the *Sefer Torah* below that was given to the Cambridge Synagogue by Trinity College where it was stored for some 300 years. It originally came from Amsterdam.

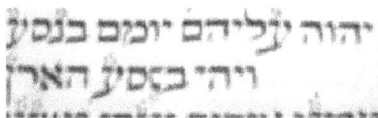
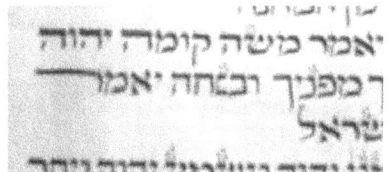
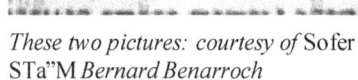

These two pictures: courtesy of Sofer STa"M *Bernard Benarroch*

And some even said there should be reversed letters in all three words.[1] Indeed, *Mishnat Avraham* reports that there are those that say it is forbidden to write [them] in the gaps between the sections as we are accustomed, but only in the middle of words - though one does not invalidate a *Sefer Torah* where they are written in the gaps of the sections in countries where one is accustomed to do this or in very old manuscripts. Thus the original custom was perhaps defined by the use of the *nun hafuchot* as brackets suggesting an error or misplaced text. Then the custom may have developed to write the *nun hafuchot* within the words and not in the gaps as suggesting that there was an error may not have been acceptable. But this is now reversed and we are back to the original method and the writing within the words invalidates a *Torah*, according to some stricter authorities. Alternatively the letters were originally reversed in the words and then this become marked in the margins, and eventually was left only in the margins. Landsofer's *Sefer Uri Or* discusses this at length looking at the *machloket* (disagreement) over the various forms of the *nun hafucha*, far too detailed to discuss here.[2]

---

1. *Mishnat Avraham* 24:13.
2. Landsofer's discussion covers 10 pages in *Uri Or* and can be found on pages 18-28 of the edition cited in the Bibliography below.

[Hebrew manuscript image]

Above: A scribe has clumsily 'corrected' the nun in binsoa *and written* nunim *in the spaces. However he has completely forgotten to 'repair' the one in* k'miton'nim. *This renders the Torah* pasul *(invalid) as you cannot have both traditions. This has been corrected below returning the scroll to the original intent of the original scribe. Photos of the Trebic Scroll Czech Memorial #158 courtesy of Soferet Avielah Barclay.*

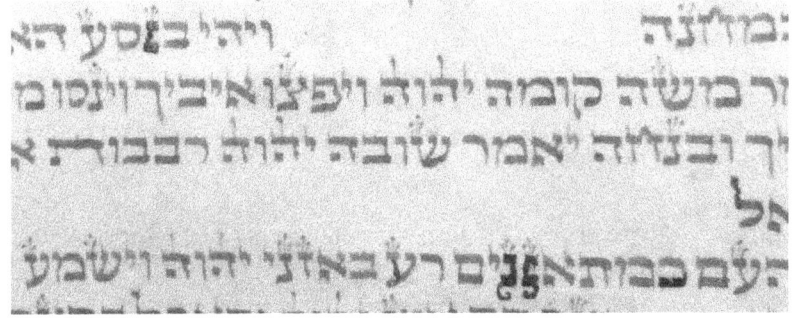

Below: This manuscript Ms. Heb. 7156=4 originally also had the reversed nunim *in the words, but a scribe has 'corrected' them and added some poorly formed ones in the spaces. The nun in* binsoa *is so poorly fixed, the base makes it look a little like a* gimel. *Image courtesy of the The National Library of Israel, Jerusalem, Israel.*

[Hebrew manuscript image]

Nonetheless, as we can see below, at least one scribe was clearly hedging his bets using all of the traditions at once.

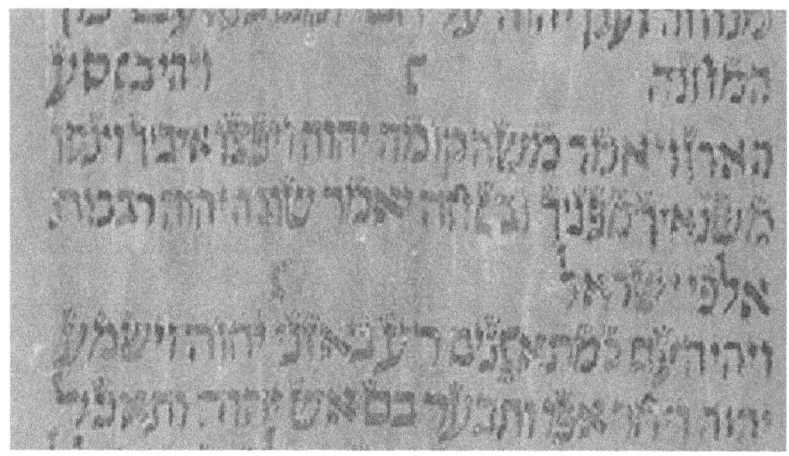

Above: the scribe of Or 1452, which was written on g'vil in the 15th Century,[1] has all three instances of the reversed nun within the three words and the two in the spaces! It seems he was familiar with all of the traditions and couldn't decide between them.

Turning to the form of the *nun*, Leitner explains that 'in the normal alphabetical order of the *alef-beis*, all the letters face away from the first letter, the *alef* - a letter that represents the Glory of *Hashem* ... so as not to stare, so to speak, directly at His Glory. When the Jewish people transgress *Hashem*'s command, He hides His *Shechinah* from us - which is the greatest possible punishment. When this happens the ... two *nuns* that face toward the right are now able to stare, as it were, directly towards the letter *alef*, because *Hashem*'s Glory is hidden.'[2]

Similarly the *Zohar*[3] discusses the *nun hafuchot* in detail in

---

1. © The British Library Board (Or 1452).
2. Leitner D, *op. cit.*, p283/4
3. The *Zohar* (lit Splendour or Radiance) is the foundational work in the literature of Jewish mystical thought known as *Kabbalah*.

section 22 referencing the different traditions of the reversed *nuns*. Indeed it would seem that the *Zohar* is describing the zig-zag 'S' shaped form when it explains that the *Shechinah* (Divine Presence) turned its face back towards Israel,

כהאי איילא דעזלתא כד איהו אזיל אהדר אפוי לאתר דנפיק וע״ד בנסוע הארון נו״ן אחסר אנפין לקבלייהו דישראל וכתבי גופא לגבי ארונה

(similar to a young deer that keeps turning her face back to the place she left when she goes forth. Therefore when the Ark set forth, the *nun* turned her face towards the children of Israel and the shoulders of her body towards the Ark).

The *Zohar* further comments that Moses saying 'Rise up God'

לא תשבוק לון אהדר אנפך לגבן כדין נו״ן אתהדר לגבייהו כגוונא דא כמאן דמהדר אנפיה למאן דרחים

([means] 'do not forsake us and turn Your face towards us' then the *nun* turned its front backwards to us like this. Like one who turns his face to someone who loves him) and that,

וכד הוה שארי ארונה למשרי כדין אהדר נו״ן אנפוי מישראל ואתהדר לגבי ארונא ובכלא אתהדר

(when the Ark began to rest, she [the *Shechinah*] turned back her face from Israel and turned her face towards the Ark.)

This would imply a similar shape where the *nun* is facing towards Israel in the next *pasuk* (*ha'am*) but the head instead turns back to face the *pasuk* about the Ark (though Israel is mentioned there too).

Many sources explain the need for these markings and it is written as a rule for the *sofer* (scribe) in the minor tractate *Sofrim* so that future generations of scribes would adhere to it,

הכותב צריך לעשות סימן בפתיחה של ויהי בנסוע הארון מלמעלה ומלמטה ...

(the scribe must make markings in the open section of [the verse] 'and when the ark travelled' above and below).[1] Above and below are interpreted by Rashi as meaning instead, מלפניו ומלאחריו (before and after.)[2]

Avot d'Rabbi Natan 34: 4 and *Shabbat* 115b also reference the need for these markings and, in this latter source, the need for them is reported as being **specific instructions from God**, תנו רבנן ויהי בנסוע פרשה זו עשה הקב"ה סימנות מלמעלה ומלמטה

(our Rabbis taught, 'and it was when the ark moved forward', the Holy One, Blessed be He made markings above and below [for this passage].)

Whilst some rabbinical texts refer to them as סימנות (markings)[3] or שיעור (measures)[4], *Midrash Mishle* and *Sifre*

---

1. *Sofrim* 6:1.
2. Sh'lomo Yitschaki (1040-1105), better known by the acronym Rashi (RAbbi SH'lomo Itschaki). Medieval French rabbi and author of the first comprehensive commentary on the *Talmud*, as well as a comprehensive commentary on the *Tanach*.
3. It is interesting to note whether the absence of any markings invalidates the *Torah*, *Keset Hasofer* 16:4 states that,
יש עוד דברים שנהגו בהם הסופרים כמו שהעתיקו איש מפי איש כמו באותיות הגדולות והקטנות והנקודות והמשונות וכל אלו למצוה ואם שינה לא פסל
(there are more things that scribes are accustomed to do. Such as old customs [spread] from man [lit. from the mouths of] to man, like the large letters and the small [letters] and the dots and the strange letters, but all these are preferences and if he erred [in them] it is not invalid.) However Landsofer in *Uri Or* argues that because these particular markings were placed there **by God** and not by individual scribal custom, then perhaps their absence would invalidate the scroll.
4. A difficult word to translate in this context but indicating a definite, legal or standard proportion or limit. Used in conjunction with שופר *shofar* (a ram's horn) in *Niddah* 26a, some have argued that this might

use the word נקוד (point)[1] and it is on this basis that Nechama Leibowitz explains that the letter *nun* is utilised since it is 'the first letter and abbreviation of the the Hebrew verb "to point" and that in order that it 'should not be mistaken for a letter it was inverted'.[2] The Encyclopedia Judaica suggests there is 'early evidence that these ... were nothing but simple dots' and it may be that these dots were over every letters of the two verses and in order to avoid having to dot every single of the 85 letters, the bracketing device of the *nun* standing for *nakud* pointed) was instituted.[3]

However as Landsofer notes in *Uri Or* the dots over the letters in the *Torah*[4] are all enumerated in a number of sources,

---

imply that the markings should be shaped liked a *shofar*. Indeed one variant reading of the minor tractate *Sofrim* 6:1 gives, הכותב צריך לעשות שיפור (the scribe must make [markings in the shape of a] *shofar*), whilst other manuscripts read שיפוד or שפוד *shipud* (an insertion). See Lieberman, S, *Hellenism in Jewish Palestine*, JTSA 1950, pp38-43 and Leiman, S, *op. cit.,* pp348-355. *Ot Y'tsiv* warns against using a *resh* or *kaf* shape, so it is possible that a *resh/shofar* like shape was used in the past.

1. *Midrash Mishle* on Proverbs 26:24 and *Sifre Bamidbar B'ha'alotcha Piska* 26 (from the *Emek HaN'tsiv* edition) respectively.
2. Leibowitz, N, *Studies in Bamidbar*, World Zionist Organisation, Jerusalem 1980, p89.
3. Indeed if it was literally 'above and below' rather than Rashi's view of 'before and after' then it is possible the original form could have resembled the dots that are above and below *luleh* in *T'hillim* 27:13 (see left).
4. There are 15 words in the *Tanach* (10 in *Torah*) which are *nakud* (dotted). One explanation is that they were inserted to call attention to some important homiletical teaching in connection with the words, but possibly they indicate that the words or letters were doubtful and are to be deleted.

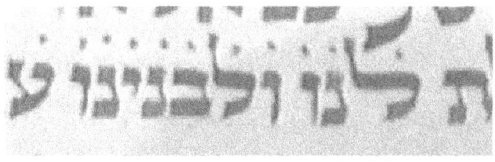

Left: An example of one of the ten occasions of dotted letters in the Torah.

particularly *Avot d'Rabi Natan* 30b[1] and this section is not noted there, so perhaps these markings can't just have been dots.

We have thus seen quite a lot of variation of opinion but the basic debate on the placing and the shape of the *nunim* is nicely summarised in both *chakirah* (example) 17^2 by Ganzfried in *Keset Hasofer* and also by the commentary *Ot Y'tsiv* on *Keset Hasofer*.

Paraphrasing Ganzfried's own *chakirah* and *M'kor Halacha* and *Biyur Halacha* on *Keset Hasofer* 15:7, we find that the reasons for placing the *nuns* in the spaces rather than in the words are three-fold:

a) they are meant to be signs and not letters and as such are not adding letters to the *Sefer Torah* which would *pasul* (invalidate) it. Hence they should be written in such a way that they aren't obviously *nuns*. This would counter the Maharshal's objection who contends that these extra letters were not the intention and instead it is preferable to have the *nuns* within reversed or upside down within the words, so as not to add extraneous letters to a *Torah*.

b) if there were inverted or reversed letters within the text then the letters wouldn't be according to their agreed halachic form (based on *Noda b'Y'hudah*) and this would *pasul* the whole *Torah*.

c) if they weren't inverted or reversed within the words of text, then even if the requirement is to do so, because the

---

D'varim *29:28 - lanu u'l'vaneynu ad (unto us and unto our children until)* has eleven dots one over each letter of the three words except the last letter dalet.

1. There are parallels in *Sifre* to *Bamidbar* 9:10, *Bamidbar Rabbah* to *Bamidbar* 3:13 and *Sofrim* 6.
2. As well as the core halachic text of *Keset Hasofer*, Ganzfried poses a set of practical questions (*chakirot*) which he then answers at length.

special letters (large small, dotted, oddly shaped etc) are only *minhagim* (customs) passed on from scribe to scribe (according to the Rambam) then the work is still *kasher* and so it doesn't matter if they were missing.

 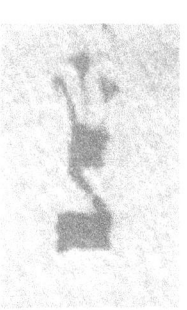

Thus the route that would appear to satisfy most opinions and not *pasul* the *Torah* is to have **inverted signs that look a bit like a *nun* in the spaces before and after the verses** and this has become accepted, though in most cases today the *nun* is probably too *nun*-like and perhaps the 'S' and 'Z' shapes shown earlier should be encouraged as a more appropriate form or marking rather than a actual letter, perhaps the *sofer* should make one of each to satisfy the both the ideas of the deer looking over its shoulder and the man kneeling in prayer.

CHAPTER 1

Though discussions over whether the marking should be a *nun*, and if so why this should be the case, and exactly what form this *nun* should take are undoubtedly worthy, this will not be the main concern of this book. Rather the question which will be answered is why such a distinctive marking should actually be necessary at all.

For, whilst there is a quite straightforward reason for this scribal oddity offered by one rabbi, there is another much more fanciful explanation from another sage which lends these two *p'sukim* a quite elevated status and one upon which this book will expand upon.

What - dare one say - is the point of the 'points'?

The most logical and frequently quoted explanation, as we have noted above, is that the verses are in the wrong place - and the signs draw attention to this. It is R. Shim'on ben Gamliel[1] who explains that the reason for the notation is that, עתירה פרשה זו שתיעקר מכאן ותכתב במקומה (in the future this section is to be removed from here and written in its

---

1. 2nd generation *Tanna* (c.10BCE-70 CE), succeeded his father Gamliel I as the *Nasi* of the *Sanhedrin* and killed by the Romans as one of the ten Jewish martyrs.

[proper] place).[1]

Its proper place according to Rav Ashi[2] in *Shabbat* 116a is בדגלים *ba-d'galim* (in the [chapter on the] banners). This, explains Silbermann[3] is after verse 17 in chapter 2,[4] which deals with 'the disposition of the Israelites according to their banners and their travel arrangements'[5] since the content of our verses is similarly about setting off and making camp.

The *Ba'al Haturim*[6] explains that the significance of the marking is to indicate that,
ועשה נוני"ן הפוכין לומר שמקומה לפני נ' פרשיות לפניה (He [God] made the inverted *nuns* to say that its [proper] place is 50 verses previous).[7] *Nun* has a numerical value of 50 and the inversion suggests that it is previous (i.e. looking backwards)

---

1. *Shabbat* 115b. Similar is found in *Sifre Bamidbar B'ha'alotcha Piska* 26.
2. 4th generation Babylonian *Amora* (352-427) who reestablished the academy at Sura and was first editor of the Babylonian *Talmud*.
3. Silbermann, A, *Pentateuch with Rashi's Commentary*, *Bamidbar*, Jerusalem, 1933, p52a.
4. Which reads,
ונסע אהל מועד מחנה הלוים בתוך המחנה כאשר יחנו כן יסעו איש על ידו לדגלים
(and the appointed tent shall set forth [with] the camp of the Levites in the midst of the [other] camps as they encamp so shall they travel [each] man in his place by their banners).
5. Soncino *Talmud*, *Shabbat* 115a note a(4). Similarly *Sofrim* also explains that it is בנסיעת הדגלים (in the journeying of the banners).
6. A commentary on the *Torah* that particularly concerns itself with scribal oddities (visual *midrash*), the *Massorah* and *Gematria* written by Jacob ben Asher, known as *Ba'al Haturim* after his main work the *Arba'ah Turim*. Born in Cologne, Germany c.1269 and most likely died in Toledo, Spain c.1343.
7. Similarly Leitner notes that 'the letter נ, with a numerical value of fifty, represents the fifty gates of wisdom, that are incorporated within the *Torah* that was housed in the Ark', Leitner D., *op. cit.*, p284. The Rokeach points out that the names of the twelve tribes contain a total of fifty letters.

to our verses proper position not after.[1] Similar is to be found in Rabbenu Bachya's[2] commentary, but Chizkuni[3] explains that,

אמר ר' יוסי בדגלים כלומר תכף אחר ונסעו הקהתים נושאי המקדש וגו'

(Rabbi Yose[4] said 'in the [section of the] banners' in order to say it is immediately after 'and the *Kohatim*, the bearers of the sanctuary set forward ...') placing it after *Bamidbar* 10:21 instead.

Milgrom suggests that their placement here instead is 'because of the association of the words for travel, *be-nos'am* (v.34) and *binso'a* (v.35), and rest, *m'nuchah* (v.33), and *u-ve-nuchah* (v.36).'[5]

Ginsburg explains that 'the dislocation of the text is also attested by the Septuagint ... [where] verses 35, 36 preceded

---

1. The *Ba'al Haturim* also adds to the idea of why the sign is a *nun* by explaining that,

   עשה נוני"ן הפוכין שרצה להעביר השבטים שאותיותהם חמשים את הירדן שהוא רחב חמשים אלא שהחטא גרם

   (He [God] placed reversed letters nun (=50) [here] because He wanted to bring the tribes whose names contain 50 letters across the Jordan river which is 50 [cubits] wide. The Jews sins prevented this from happening.) And this explains why the letters are reversed, because they are looking backward to the preceding *parshiyot* (sections) and therefore one would not think in error that they would be referring to a place 50 *parshiyot* onwards. It is worth noting that from the end of our passage to the verse *Bamidbar* 2:17 is actually only 49 verses. However '*Or Torah* (cited in *Minchas Shai* and *Tikkun Sofrim* [Dubnai] reports seeing two ancient *Torah* scrolls which had a paragraph break between 10:21 and 10:22. Perhaps the *Ba'al Haturim* includes that *parashah* in his count' thus making 50 (*Ba'al Haturim op. cit.*, p1473).
2. Bachya ben Asher ibn Halawa , mid-thirteenth century - 1340, Spain.
3. Chez'kiah ben Manoah (13th century), France, known as the Chizkuni.
4. 4th generation *Yerushalmi Amora* (320-350 C.E.) head of the Academy at Tiberias.
5. Milgrom, J, *The JPS Torah Commentary-Numbers* JPS, Philadelphia/New York 1990, p81.

verse 34, so that the order of the verses is Numb. X 35, 36, 34 and [for him] this seems to be the proper place for the two verses.'[1]

This misplacement could be the result of an early scribal error that was then noted by the rabbis by the original dots, we have already mentioned. This in itself is striking as throughout Jewish history extreme care has been taken to preserve the Torah text and avoid such errors, particularly one of this magnitude. The two *nuns* were thus added to identify the 'mistake' without having to change the text, something that would have been unthinkable given the general agreement that the received text not be tampered with.[2]

Certainly Ginsburg notes that 'these inverted letters or their equivalents are also among the earliest signs by which the Sopherim (*sic*) designed to indicate the result of their textual criticism' and that 'they are simply intended to take the place of our modern brackets to mark that the passages thus bracketed are transposed.'[3] Tov, as we have alreday seen made a similar statement.

R. Shim'on ben Gamliel, however, does not perceive this as an *accidental* error. Instead he contends that this was entirely deliberate, and remarks,

למה כתבה כאן כדי להפסיק בין פורענות ראשונה לפרענות שנייה

(and why is it written here, in order to divide (provide a break) between the first punishment and the second

---

1. Ginsburg, C D, *op. cit.*, p343.
2. This tradition was eventually 'fixed by the Masoretes ... and the text followed today is that of Aaron Ben-Asher who worked ... in the first half of the tenth century' (Ed. Posner, R. & Ta-Shema, I, *The Hebrew Book - An Historical Survey*, p25.)
3. Ginsburg, C D, *op. cit.*, p342. He also suggests that the *nuns* used in conjunction with sections of *T'hillim* 107 are similarly out of place and suggests they could be moved to the end of the psalm and also suggests that verse 40 should precede verse 39 to make more sense (p344).

punishment). He further explains what these are,

פרענות שנייה מאי היא ויהי העם כמתאוננים פרענות ראשונה ויסעו מהר וא"ר חמא בר' חנינא שסרו מאחרי ה'

(what is the second punishment? 'And the people were as murmurers ...' (*Bamidbar* 11:1) [and the] first punishment 'and they moved away from the mountain of the Lord' (*ibid*. 10:30) [which] R. Chamma[1] said in the name of R. Chanina[2] [meant] that they turned away from following after God).[3]

Dividing the punishments with these verses, it is argued, would 'relieve the gloomy affect that would otherwise be produced'[4] and allow Israel to reflect on a more promising state of affairs where their enemies are scattered before them and they would be victorious.

The future return of our verses to their proper position, one assumes, refers to the arrival of the Messiah who, amongst the many tasks he will have to perform, is to sort out all the scribal problems within the *Torah* texts explaining or removing the enlarged, reduced and additional letters, copyists mistakes etc. Thus, Rabbeynu Bachya states,

עתידה שתעקר ממקומה לימות המשיח שיהיו כל הפורעניות בטלים ויצר הרע בטל

(in the future that it will be removed from its place in the days of the Messiah where all punishments will cease and the evil

---

1. Father of R. Chanina - see note immediately below.
2. 1st generation *Yerushalmi Amora* (220-250 C.E.), R. Chanina b. Chamma was head of the Council of Sepphoris.
3. *Shabbat* 116a. Interestingly enough, *Minchat Shai* on *Tehillim* 107:23 explains the use of the use of an inverted *nun* there as implying a turning away, citing *Y'shayah* 1:4 נדרו אחור (*they turned backwards*). Indeed, 'after [these sins] there is a third sin, murmuring for meat. In Judaism three things in a row make a 'chazukah' (a permanent situation), in this case designated the Jews to be permanent sinners' (Gershon, A G, *The Weekly Torah*, Chabad in Cyberspace 1996). The avoidance of this three-in-a-row by having our inserted passage thus takes on even greater significance.
4. *Soncino Talmud*, *Shabbat* 116a, note a(5).

inclination will cease.)¹ Rashi who favours the *p'shat* (straightforward explanation) adopts R. Ashi's explanation in his commentary and many other commentators repeat it, with the notable exception of Sforno (see below).

However it is the *Baraita*² that we find quoted directly above this in the *Talmud*, which is much more fanciful and which lends an elevated status to the verses.

ר' אומר לא מן השם הוא אלא מפני שספר חשוב הוא בפני עצמו
(Rabbi (Y'hudah Hanasi)³ said it is not [because it is in the wrong place], rather because it is an <u>important</u> book standing by itself).⁴

It is worth noting that *Midrash Mishley* on *Mishley* 26:24 preserves a parallel text, which differs slightly and renders instead, **רבי אמר ספר היה בפני עצמו ונגנז** which has been read as 'Rabbi said this was a book by itself and it was **withdrawn**'. The word **ונגנז** has led to some speculation that it was the remnant of another apocryphal book containing the prophesies of Eldad and Medad⁵ but Leiman demonstrates this

---

1. See also Soncino *Talmud op. cit.*, note a(8).
2. A *Baraita* (meaning 'outside' designates a tradition from a *Tanna* not incorporated in the *Mishnah*.
3. A 6th generation *Tanna*, born 138 CE, died c.219 CE and regarded traditionally and by modern scholars as the redactor of the *Mishnah* the basis of the Oral Law. He is mostly known in the rabbinical writing simply as **רבי**, 'Rabbi' *par excellence*, indicating his importance and status.
4. Shabbat 115a. *Sifre Bamidbar B'ha'alotcha Piska* 26 also gives Rabbi as the sage, but does not say it is **important**, only that it stands alone.
5. Heschel in particular brings this view that this book of Eldad and Medad would have comprised some 400 verses (based on a Christian source). He also brings a fragment of poetry that is preserved in *B'reshit Rabbah* by R. Nappaha (2nd generation *Amora*) that he claims was part of the lost book and is reportedly the Israelites reply to Moses' statement "Arise, O Lord." It reads,
'Raise yourself up, O acacia wood,
Carry your splendour like a banner,

erroneous assumption by showing that ונגנז should be read in the *niphal* particle. This implies that Rabbi is referring to the 'the technical term ... by which sacred objects which have outlived their usefulness are ... stored away or buried in a manner which allows them to decompose naturally'.[1] By employing ונגנז he is thus only indicating that 'Num. l0:35-36 formed not only an independent book but one, sufficiently large enough to qualify for, [and] indeed to require, *genizah*.'[2]

This reasoning is echoed in *Yadayim* 3:5 and *Sifre Bamidbar B'ha'alotcha Piska* 26 and forms the basis of an halachic ruling regarding the sanctity of written texts,

מגילה שכתוב בה פ"ה אותיות כפרשה ויהי בנסוע הארון מטמא את הידים

(a scroll that has written in it 85 letters as in the the section *'and it was when the Ark went forward ... '* renders unclean the hands). The very act of making the hands unclean means this constitutes a book which is holy, requiring *genizah* and to be saved from fire [on the Sabbath].)[3]

In further support of this radical idea of only two verses constituting an <u>entire book</u> of the *Torah*, *Shabbat* 115b provides a dictum by a later rabbi which shows how another biblical book 'proves' Y'hudah Hanasi's view,

---

You who are decorated with gold,
And are enshrined in the royal palace
(Shrouded between the cherubim)
And adorned with the most precious of ornaments.' (Heschel, A J, *Heavenly Torah*, Continuum, NY, 2007, p645) which is interesting as it focuses on the Israelites responding to the Ark rather than God. Hertz, however, suggests that they may have been taken from another source, possibly from the Book of the Wars of the Lord (Hertz, J H, *Pentateuch & Haftorahs*, Soncino Press, 2nd Ed., London 1987, p.613.)

1. Leiman, *op. cit.*, p354. *Megillah* 26b deals with the disposal of religious appurtenances in detail.
2. *Ibid.*
3. See *Shabbat* 115a, כל כתבי הקדש מצילין אותו מפני הדליקה (all holy writings are to be saved from fire).

דא"ר שמואל בר נחמן א"ר יונתן חצבה עמידיה שבעה אלו שבעה ספרי תורה

(that R. Shmuel b. Nachman[1] said in the name of R. Yonatan[2] 'she [wisdom] has hewn out her seven pillars' (*Mishley* 9:1), these [pillars] being the seven books of the law.) 'Wisdom' in Proverbs is often understood as referring to the *Torah* and 'since this section is a separate book, the portions of Numbers proceeding and following it are also separate books; hence there are seven in all.'[3]

Given the pressures of a modern world it is impossible for most people to find the time to offer a detailed commentary on a biblical book,[4] but, if we accept Rabbi's explanation at its face value that these two verses constitute an entire, separate book of the Law, this is something that one could do. Moreover, returning to the first version of the *Baraita*, we understand it to be an **important** book, and thus it must be worthy of such comment.

The 17th century biblical commentator, *K'lei Yakar*[5] notes that,

כי יפלא ממך דבר   לאמר הרי עיקר התורה למצותיה נתנה ובספר זה אין רמז לשום מצוה

(one may question you [as to why it is a book on its own]

---

1. 3rd generation *Yerushalmi Amora* (320-359 C.E.). In the Babylonian *Talmud* he is mentioned as Nachmani.
2. Probably R. Yonatan ben Eleazar whose pupil was Sh'muel b. Nachman.
3. *Soncino Talmud, Shabbat* 115b note a(3). See also Hertz's comment to *Bamidbar* 34-36, *op. cit.*, p614. The books would be *B'reshit, Sh'mot, Vayikra, Bamidbar,* **Binsoa**, *Ha'am, D'varim*.
4. The *Talmud* does offer an alternative book in the form of the portion of Balak, which it claims was also a separate work, though still written by Moses (*Bava Batra* 14b) and also **important** in that it was considered as being suitable for daily use in the service, as part of the *Shema* (*B'rachot* 12b). Accepting both this and our premise above would give us no less than **nine** books of Moses!
5. Written by Sh'lomo Ephraim ben Aaron Luntschitz (1550-1619).

saying the root of the *Torah* is in its commandments but in this book there is no allusion for the sake of a commandment.)

In answer to his question therefore, below are some thoughts on what would be the fifth book of the 'Seven books of Moses' - *Sefer Binsoa* (the book of *Binsoa*)[1] - why it might be considered important and what lessons it holds for us today.

---

[1] It was the agreed methodology that each *sedra* (portion) receives its name from the first significant word within that portion.

CHAPTER 2

Information

Relationship Status:
In a relationship with GOD

There are many ways to translate any given Hebrew passage.

Plaut/JPS, for example, translate our first verse as 'When the ark was to set out, Moses would say 'Advance O Lord! May your enemies be scattered and may your foes flee before you.'[1]

This translation unlike that give above (page 5) suggests that the Ark did not set forward until Moses had said his piece, almost as if he was giving an order. It is around this issue of the Ark setting off apparently at Moses' command that the sages encounter their first difficulty with the text. They ask, ויאמר משה קומה ה' וכתוב אחר אומר על פי ה' יחנו וע"פ ה' יסעו כיצד יתקיימו ב' כתובים ('and Moses said 'arise Lord'' and another verse (*Bamidbar* 9:20-23) says 'by the word of the Lord they encamped and by the word of the Lord they journeyed' - how can these two [seemingly contradictory] verses co-exist?)[2]

---

1. Plaut, W G, *op. cit.*, p1091, Milgrom, J, *op. cit.*, p81.
2. *Sifre Bamidbar B'ha'alotcha Piska* 26.

Since it appears that Moses is ordering God to move forward the *Pesichta d'Rav Kahana*[1] takes this as the ultimate demonstration of a partnership between Moses and God, one which gives Moses considerable authority and status,

איש האלהים א"ר יונתן אישה יקימנו ואישה יפירנו אישה יקימנו ויהי בנסוע ואישה יפירנו ובנוחה יאמר שובה ה' רבבות אלפי ישראל

('[Moses] the man of God' (*T'hillim* 90:1) - R. Yonatan said [this can be read along side the verse 'her spouse may cause her to rise up and her spouse may cause her to void her vow' (*Bamidbar* 30:14).[2] 'Her spouse causes her to rise up' [witness] 'and when the Ark went forward [Moses said arise]' and 'her spouse causes her to void her vow' witness 'and when it rested he said 'return Lord [to] the myriads of thousands of Israel'.)[3]

איש can mean spouse as well as man, and R. Yonatan 'took the phrase not only as signifying Moses' espousing of the *Shechinah*, but also as intimating that Moses had the authority over the *Shechinah* that a spouse had over his wife'[4] - the parallel being made between the words 'rise up' in 'her spouse may cause her to rise up ...' and Moses' command 'Rise up!' in our verse, with a deliberate reading of the object of the verb applying to the woman herself rather than the vows or oaths that it refers to in context.

This sort of interpretation, complimentary as it might be to Moses, is nonetheless somewhat dangerous as it gives an inordinate amount of power to the human part of the

---

1. One of the oldest collections of Aggadic *midrash*.
2. In context this would normally be translated 'her husband may let [her vows] stand or her husband may make it void' (Cohen, A, *Soncino Chumash*, p957).
3. *Pesichta d'Rav Kahana,* Supplement 1, section 9.
4. Paraphrase of the translation from Montefiore, C G & Loewe, H, *A Rabbinic Anthology*, Schocken Books, 1974.

relationship. In allowing man to 'order' God around *kivyachol* (as it were) one need only move a small step forward to provide the rationalisation for some to defend the unspeakable horrors committed in the name of God by religious fanatics throughout the centuries and today. These people are dictating their own agenda to God rather than submitting to His will.

For us, like the majority of the sages, the idea of Moses being able to tell God what to do is an anathema, and a different explanation is required. At its simplest one needs only to read the text at its most literal, to remove the problem, 'and when the Ark was travelling, Moses would [then] say 'Rise up O Lord ...,' i.e. the Ark begins its travels, בנסוע (in the travelling of) and only then would Moses react by making his statement.[1] And, of course, it is by God's will, and not that of Moses that the Ark moves. The cause and effect suggested by the Plaut/JPS translation is reversed.

The Sages in *Sifre* also provide an explanation that similarly gives honour to Moses, but in a different and, arguably, more acceptable manner,

משל למלך בשר ודם שאמר לעבדו הנראה שתעמידני בשביל שאני הולך ליתן ירושה לבני

(these [verses] can be compared to a king of flesh and blood who said to his servant it appears [to others as though] that you cause me to stand when I go to give an inheritance to my son.)[1]

The inheritance is, of course, the Land of Israel and the

---

1. It is worth noting that Neusner's rendition of the *niphal* form הנראה results in the poor translation, 'see to it that you arrange things for me that I may go and give my son an inheritance' (Neusner, J, *Sifre to Numbers*, Vol II, Scholars Press, Atlanta, 1986, p71). This suggests that the King had to vocalise his wishes, when in fact the reverse is the case, with the servant knowing his master's requirements so well that he takes the active role without any express command, thus appearing to others to be in control.

inheritors are the people of Israel. Moses' role here is as a servant, but a very valued and trusted one who is so 'in tune' with his master's needs that to the outsider the perception is that the servant is ordering around the master. A similar relationship can perhaps be witnessed in the *Torah* between Potiphar and Joseph, where the servant is so trusted that he can act with the master's consent even before the master has made his will known explicitly.[1] Hirsch explains that whilst it may have appeared otherwise, 'neither starting nor coming to rest occurred at Moses' orders and yet Moses accompanied both by his demands, as though what had already happened was now to do so' and suggests the lesson here is that one should 'greet every decision of God as if it were one's own decision.'[2]

These same sages then offer an alternative explanation, assigning Moses yet another role,

ד"א למה הדבר דומה למלך בשר ודם שהיה מתהלך בדרך ונהג אוהבו עמו כשהוא נוסע אומר איני נוסע עד שיבא אוהבי וכשהוא חונה אומר איני חונה עד שיבא אוהבי נמצאת מקיים על פי משה יחנו ונמצאת מקיים על פי ה' יחנו ועל פי משה יסעו ועל פי ה' יסעו

(Another explanation - to what can this thing be compared? To a king of flesh and blood who was walking by the way and his loved one was leading along with him. When he [the king]

---

1. ויפקדהו על ביתו וכל יש לו נתן בידו (and [Potiphar] appointed [Joseph] over his household, and all that he had, he put into his control (*Bereshit* 39:4)). R. Yochanan makes a similar comment when explaining the relative greatness of R. Chaninah,

   אמר לה לאו הוא אלא דומה כעבד לפני המלך ואני דומה כשר לפני המלך

   (he said to her, I (Yochanan) am like a royal minister who enters only with permission, while he (Chanina) is like a servant who has the run of the house). *B'rachot* 34b (paraphrase translation from Ed. Katz, S, *Hamaayan* #10:32, Internet, 1996, based on Rashi's commentary).
2. Hirsch, S R, *The Pentateuch - translation and commentary*, Judaica Press, Gateshead 1989, p169/1702.

was to travel he says "I am not travelling until my loved one comes" and when he was to make camp, he said, "I am not making camp until my loved one comes". Thus we find standing 'by the word of Moses they encamped' alongside 'by the word of the Lord they encamped' and 'by the word of Moses they travelled' and 'by the word of the Lord, they travelled'.)[1]

Two key words here are נהג and אוהבי. Neusner[2] translates נהג simply as 'went' whereas the actual verb suggests some sort of leading or guiding[3] as if the king's favourite is in partnership and involved almost jointly in the leading of whatever entourage is following the king, though at all times it is made clear that the king is allowing this. אוהבי has been translated above as 'my loved one' however could merely be a good friend or, as Neusner suggests, taking this 'walking by the way' in a more military vein as an 'ally'.[4] Following on from the previous *mashal*, we might even take this to imply the king's own son, but whichever, there is a clearly a very special relationship based on love or very good friendship here.

The rabbis have thus interpreted this verse to show Moses as a trusted servant; a loved one (perhaps a child or very special friend) or as the spouse of the Eternal.

These ideas will seem instantly familiar to us as they reflect the traditional roles of the Jew in relation to God.

We call God *Adonai* (Lord) or *Melech* (King), and as such we are His servants. We refer to God as *Avinu* (our Father) and we are his loved ones, His children, *b'ney Yisrael*. Moreover,

---

1. *Sifre Bamidbar B'ha'alotcha Piska* 26.
2. Neusner, *op. cit.*, p71.
3. Jastrow, M, *Dictionary of the Targumim, Talmud Babli, Yerushalmi and Midrashic Literature*, Judaic Press, New York, 1989, p880.
4. Neusner, *ibid.*

the writings and liturgy are full of references of the marriage of God to the people of Israel.[1] Indeed *Shir Hashirim* (Song of Songs) has been interpreted as a whole by the *Midrash*, *Targum* and medieval Jewish commentators as 'depicting the spiritual marriage between God and Israel after the Revelation at Sinai.'[2]

Moses in this verse, acts as the consummate role model to show us the different relationships we can have with God, perhaps ascending in our status as we draw closer to Him.

We can be God's servant, doing God's will but in such a way that it appears to others that we are in command. This is perhaps the ultimate answer to the question of free will. Man appears to be doing something under his control but in reality the righteous man is acting out the will of God - they just happily co-incide. Rabbi Gamliel[3] presents this view strongly in *Pirkey Avot* when he states,

עשה רצונו כרצונך כדי שיעשה רצונך כרצונו (Do His will as if it was your will, that He may do your will as if it was His will)[4] for 'as we turn to God, God turns to us. It is an entirely reciprocal relationship.'[5]

If we are able to accept God's will as our own, we can be granted the position of ally or loved one, protected by God, yet expected to actively assist God in the guidance of His

---

1. See *Hoshea* 2:4, 21, *Y'shayah* 62:5, *Yirm'yah* 2:2 and *Y'chezkiel* 16:8 for examples from the *Tanach*.
2. Ed. Cohen, A, *The Five Megilloth*, Soncino Press, London, 1975, px.
3. R. Gamliel, a first generation *Amora* and son of Rabbi Y'hudah Hanasi (see above).
4. *Avot* 2:4. In *Eicha* 3:37 we read מי זה אמר ותהי ה' לא צוה (who [ever] said something and it came to be unless the Lord had ordained it). Similarly Moses' instruction only comes to pass because God willed it.
5. Plaut, W G & Stern, C, *The Haftarah Commentary*, UAHC, New York, 1997, p334. This concept will reappear when considering the ideas inherent in the second *pasuk* regarding 'return'.

entourage [i.e. the world].[1] God requires us to help Him out, to meet him half way. This is perhaps echoed in another famous *midrash* involving a king-prince/father-son relationship and an echo of travelling and return,

[דבר אחר] שובה ישראל עד ה' אלהיך לבן מלך שהיה רחוק מאביו מהלך מאה יום אמרו לו אוהביו חזור אצל אביך אמר להם איני יכול שלח אביו ואמר לו הלך מה שאתה יכול לפי כחך (ואם) [ואני] בא אצלך (כשאר) הדרך כך אמר להם הקדוש ברוך הוא שובו אלי ואשובה אליכם

([Another interpretation] on 'return Israel unto the Lord your God.' [This can be compared] to the king's son who was far from his father - one hundred days journey. His friends said to him, "Return to you father." He said, "I cannot." His father sent to him and said to him, "Come back as far as your strength permits, and if so, I will come to you the rest of the way." So said the Holy One, Blessed be He to them (Israel) 'Return to me and I will return to you' (*Malachi* 3:7).)[2]

This *midrash* is usually mentioned in the context of repentance but is equally appropriate to our ideas of a joint venture between God and man and even though we may not always have the strength, it is nonetheless beholden upon us to assist as far as we can.

At the apex, we can even view ourselves as the spouse of God, almost an equal in a relationship that is akin to marriage. However, whilst the *Pesichta d'Rav Kahana* suggests that Moses was in the apparently commanding position of the husband (although that traditional view clearly does not hold true today) this would suggest we can order God about and

---

1. According to Pelcovitz, it is Sforno's view that 'בחירה חפשית (freedom of choice) and Divine Providence are interwoven. The man who strives to imitate God and attempts to adopt His will as his own has utilized the gift of free will as intended by God and therefore deserves to be under His protection'. (Pelcovitz, R, *Sforno - Commentary on the Torah*, Mesorah Publications, 1997, pxiv)
2. *Pesichta Rabati* 44.

use Him to our own ends, as indeed many people have done. This is, however, a negative interpretation that we should guard against and if we wish to use the imagery of marriage, perhaps a more modern view of it being a partnership with a common goal is a better one.[1]

So far we have considered Moses' statement as an order to God, because it appears in the emphatic imperative form, however if we look at it rather as a petition that God, in the form of the *Shechinah* (Divine Presence) will arise and travel along with the Ark and the people, the difficulties disappear.

Certainly *Or Chayim*[2] to *Bamidbar* 10:35 explains that, וכיון צשה בדה להתפלל (it was Moses' intention through this [statement] to pray), whilst *Da'at Z'kenim*[3] refers to this section as תפלת הדרך שלהם (their prayer for the journey). Milgrom too suggests that 'the Song is only a prayer', since 'the imperative "Arise," "Rest" are not written in the usual form *kum, shuv,* but are lengthened to *kumah, shuvah* and thus may be expressing a wish."[4]

This petitionary stance is perhaps more in keeping with the character of the humble Moses[5] than the more warlike

---

1. Similarly Plaut and Stern come to the same conclusion in their essay on *Hoshea*, though from a different direction. Here God is the master in the marriage and Israel merely the adulterous wife. They note that this view of 'male-female relationships ... [is] now being increasingly abandoned in Western Societies ... In theology too, the Eternal - though Sovereign - is seen increasingly in terms of partnership: God needs us to perfect the world, even as we need God to make our lives whole and meaningful.' (Plaut, W G & Stern, C, *The Haftarah Commentary, op. cit.*, p333/4).
2. Chaim ben Moses ibn Attar, known as the Ohr Chayyim, born Morocco 1696 and died in Jerusalem 1743.
3. A compendium of Torah commentary originating with the Tosafists of the 13th century, disciples of Rashi. It was first printed in 1783 in Livorno.
4. Milgrom, J, *op. cit.*, p375.
5. See, for example, Moses at the burning bush,

invocation that would have perhaps have been favoured by his successor Joshua. According to some scholars, the section from *Bamidbar* 10:29-36 incorporating our verses is the first time that we have heard from the author of J[1] since the Golden Calf incident. Bloom notes that in this section we see a 'very human request [made by] Moses to his father-in-law [Jethro] as he desperately seeks a guide through the wilderness' and 'in returning to J's Moses we are back with a prophet who knew his limitations all too well, and who moves us not by sublime grandeur but by a sense that he will never overcome his reluctance to lead.'[2] As well as petitioning Jethro, perhaps Moses in our verses is also pleading with God in a fallible human way. The radical translation Rosenberg offers is thus less overtly militaristic, with 'scatter' and 'flee' being replaced with 'disappear' and 'fade'. Moreover, in his words, verse 36 sees a plea to a God who is all, from Moses who recognises he, and indeed all Israel is as nothing,

He translates, 'Now look: as the ark set out; Moses says, 'Arise Yahweh, your enemies disappear like stars; your haters fade before you.' When it rests, he says, 'come back, you who embody Israel's countless thousands.''[3]

Even though the Ark is the traditional resting place,[4] God's footstool, there was perhaps no guarantee that the *Shechinah* would remain with the Ark and thus with the people protecting them.[5] Indeed Rashi, based on *Tachuma Vayakhel*

מי אנכי כי אלך אל פרעה (who am I that I should go to Pharaoh ... (*Sh'mot* 3:11).)

1. J or 'Yawhest', the title given to what scholars who subscribe to the documentary hypothesis believe is the oldest strand in the Pentateuch, probably composed c. 950-900 BCE in Jerusalem.
2. Rosenberg, D & Bloom, H, *The Book of J*, Faber and Faber 1990, p220.
3. *Ibid.*
4. 'Originally, the Ark seemed to have been a portable throne on which, it was believed, Yahweh was invisibly enthroned' (Anderson, B, *The Living World of the Old Testament*, Longman 1998, p116).
5. Milgrom notes that 'Moses petitions the Lord to arise from His throne and attack the enemy and then to return to His throne on the

explains that, שהיה מקדים לפניהם מהלך שלשת ימים (that [the Ark] was travelling three days ahead of them) and that Moses is actually imploring God to, עמוד והמתן לנו ואל תתרחק יותר (stand and wait for us and not go any further).[1]

Moreover, such an assertion, out loud to the people would make it perfectly clear that God was not the Ark, but separate from it.[2] The potentially idolatrous Israelites (witness the Golden Calf incident) would perhaps need reminding of each time the Ark set forth that, holy though it was, it was not what they followed, but rather it was God. Similarly by making a plea that God accompany them on their travels, Moses was reminding the people that whilst he may look like he was in charge, he was actually as helpless as they without God's constant aid.

Yalkut Shimoni to verse 35, however, suggests that the Israelites did appreciate this, but would not follow Moses until he had proved to them that God's presence was with them, בא משה אמר לישראל עמדו סעו הרי השכינה בארון אמרו ליה אין אנו מאמינים אמר קומה ה' והארון מזדעז לכך היו מאמינים (Moses came and said to Israel, stand and travel, behold the *Shechinah* is in/with the Ark. They said to him, we do not

---

Ark-cherubim after the battle is over. There is no assurance that He will do either.' (Milgrom, J, *op. cit.*, p375)

1. Rashi's commentary to verse 35.
2. The 'Mosaic religion strictly vetoed the worship of Yawhweh in the form of a visible image. In this respect, the religion of Israel differed radically from the religions of other peoples, who represented the deity's presence by ... bearing the image of the deity in festive processions' (Milgrom, J, *op cit.,* p117). 'We know that other nomadic peoples carried similar portable sanctuaries on their migrations, though these sanctuaries were more like sedan chairs in which their gods could be borne along in state' (Barthel, M, *What the Bible Really Says*, Wings Books, 1992, p126), so this would have been a very real danger for the Israelites who may have supposed their Ark was no different to other such representations.

believe. [Moses] said, 'Rise up Lord ...' and the Ark shook,[1] therefore they believed.)

Indeed one is left to wonder too if the *Kohanim* (priests) carried the Ark or whether it, in some supernatural way, moved itself and then they ran to take up their positions and appear to carry it! And indeed Sforno does conclude that this miraculous event did occur, in that the Ark was in fact three days in front of the Israelites and moved of its own accord,

להבטיח הדרך מן הנחשים והעקרבים וזולתם אבל בשאר המסעות היה הארון נוסע בתוך המחנות כשאר מסע בני קהת

(to secure the way from serpents and scorpions and other [things] besides them. However, on all other journeys the Ark travelled in the midst of the camps similar to the other carryings of the sons of *K'hat* ...)[2]

---

1. The Stone *Chumash* translates 'When the Ark would journey', perhaps implying no human intervention, but perhaps a suggestion of the of the miraculous sequence of events, though is offered by the *Targum Yonatan ben Uzziel* which shows the Cloud of Glory as the active force. It reads,

והוה כד הוה בעי למיטל ארונה הוה עננה מקפל וקאים ולא הוה נטיל עד דמשה הוה קאי בצלו מצלי ובעי רחמין מן קדם יי וכן אמר אתגלי כדון מימרא דיי בתקוף רוגזך ויתבדרון בעלי דבביהון דעמך ולא יהוי לסנאיהון ריגל למיקום משה אתגלי יי ויתבדרון סנאיך ויעקרון בעלי דבבך מן קדמך

(And it was when the Ark should go forward, the Cloud gathered itself together and stood still, not going on, until Moses, standing in prayer, prayed and supplicated mercy from before the Lord, and said, 'Let the Word of the Lord be now revealed in the power of Your anger, that the adversaries of Your people maybe scattered; and let not the banner of those who hate them be uplifted before You. But when the Ark would rest, the Cloud gathered itself together and stood, but did not overspread, until Moses, standing in prayer, prayed and besought mercy from before the Lord, saying, 'Return now, You Word of the Lord, in the goodness of Your mercy, and lead Your people Israel, and let the glory of Your *Shechinah* dwell among them, and [Your] mercy with the myriads of the house of Jacob, and with the multitudes of the thousands of Israel.)

2. Pelcovitz notes that by this Sforno means that 'the Ark of the covenant

Perhaps the Ark would miraculously waver back and forth, but it would not actually journey from its place until Moshe said 'Arise God'.

To a certain extent this also reflects our relationship with God today. We too have an Ark in the synagogue and we too petition God to be present during our prayers and in our lives and we ask Him to perform miracles on our behalf, but there is no guarantee. We sometimes do not believe that God is with us or listens to our prayers. We doubt even though we are told otherwise by our spiritual leaders. Moreover we can too easily get caught up in the ritual elements of our religion and forget that the physical Ark and the physical *Torah* scroll itself are just symbols and the overall purpose of our faith is to define our relationship with God and with the ideas and direction that His words contain.[1]

Whilst we may sometimes foolishly think otherwise, God moves and we move with Him. Whereas our previous understanding of Moses' 'ordering' God around led us to enjoy a quite lofty relationship with God, here we, like the Moses of J, recognise that in fact we are nothing without God's support and more appropriate would be the *mishna* from *Avot* that follows directly after 2:4 quoted above, ואל תאמן בעצמך עד יום מותך (and trust not in your self until the day of your death,)[2] rather God is the source of your intelligence, wealth, happiness etc. and we are merely His

---

went miraculously before the Israelites without being carried by the Kehatitics' (Pelcovitz, R., *Sforno - Commentary on the Torah*, Artscroll Mesorah Series 1997).

1. Simon Rocker wrote in the *Jewish Chronicle* (September 5th 1997) on the need to 'restore God to the centre of Jewish life', noting that 'Jews appear to practice their religion more than they believe in it' and that in the past 'it might have been presumed that the however backsliding Jews were in their observance, most still subscribed to some idea of Deity. But that can no longer be taken for granted. For many Jews, God has become a disappearing act.' A worrying thought indeed.
2. *Avot* 2:5

servants and the grateful recipients of His bounty.

Moses' statements in these two verses, whether perceived as an 'order', a simple statement, a request or a plea thus show a number of relationships we may have with God and we may experience each of them at different times - the multiplicity of roles we may play with regard to God is extensive, as this *piyyut* from the *Yom Kippur* service demonstrates,

אנו בניך ואתה אבינו	כי אנו עמך ואתה אלקינו
אנו קהלך ואתה חלקנו	אנו עבדיך ואתה אדונינו
אנו צאנך ואתה רוענו	אנו נחלתך ואתה גורלנו
אנו פעלתך ואתה יוצרנו	אנו כרמך ואתה נוטרנו
אנו סגלתך ואתה קרובנו	אנו רעיתך ואתה דודנו
אנו מאמיריך ואתה מאמירנו	אנו עמך ואתה מלכנו

> For we are Your people and You are our God.
> We are Your children and You are our father.
> We are Your servants and You are our master.
> We are Your community and You are our portion.
> We are Your inheritance and You are our destiny.
> We are Your flock and You are our shepherd.
> We are Your vineyard and You are our keeper.
> We are Your work and You are our creator.
> We are Your beloved and You are our friend.
> We are Your own and You are our nearest.
> We are You people and You are our king.
> We are the people known to You
> and You are the God made known by us.

At times we can feel lofty and important - the partners of God, at others, merely servants trying to understand His will.

Perhaps this is neatly encapsulated in a famous saying from Rabbi Bunam of Pzhysha,[1]

---

1. Rabbi Simcha Bunam Bonhart of Peshischa, Poland (1765-1827).

מצוה היא על כל אדם שיהיו לו שני כיסים בכליו כדי שיוכל
להושיט ידו אל האחד או אל השני לפי הצרך בכיסו הימיני ימצה
את המלם למעני נברא העולם ובשמאלי ימצא עפר ואפר אנכי

(it is incumbent upon each man that he have two pockets in his garments, so that he is able to reach his hand into one or the other according to his needs. In his right pocket he will find the words 'for my sake the world was created',[1] and in the left 'I am but dust and ashes').

The best we can hope for is the unequal partnership and we should be grateful for that.

---

1. Based on *Sanhedrin* 4:5, לפיכך כל אחד ואחד חיב לומר בשבילי נבר העול (therefore everyone is bound to say 'for me the world was created').

Chapter 3

Rather than look at the our verses in linear fashion, to draw out the next element it is necessary to move to the very end of the text. The last phrase of our verses is difficult to translate without having to add in an additional word that is not in the Hebrew.

Literally the verse reads, שובה ה' רבבות אלפי ישראל (Return Lord - myriads of thousands of Israel). Most translators deal with this by adding in the words 'unto the',[1] myriads, but there are other ways of translating which we will consider later.

Sifre draws on the echo of this text to be found in *T'hillim* 68:18 (which incidentally is near to the parallel text of God rising and scattering the foe)[2] to explain, ובנחה יאמר [וגו'] מגיד הכתוב שאין שכינה שורה למעלה אלא באלפים ורבבות שנ' רכב אלהים רבותים אלפי שנאן (תהילים ס"ח) וכשם שאין שכינה שורה למעלה אלא באלפים ורבבות כך אין שכינה שורה למטה אלא באלפים ורבבות ('And when it rested, he would say ...' The verse teaches that the Divine Presence rests above [in heaven] only for the

---
1. Leibowitz notes that this 'presents a syntactical difficulty. The Hebrew verb: *shuv* is usually an intransitive verb implying return, and yet it is followed [here] by the phrase "many thousands of Israel" as a direct object.' (Leibowitz, *op.cit*, p91).
2. *T'hillim* 68:2 reads, יקום אלהים יפוצו אויביו וינוסו משנאיו מפניו (Let God arise, let His enemies be scattered and let those that hate Him flee before Him.)

thousands and myriads, as it says 'the Chariots of God are myriads, thousands of angels' (*T'hillim* 68:18), and just as the Divine Presence does not rest above for thousands and myriads, so it only rests below [on earth] for thousands and myriads.)[1]

Rashi, based on *Y'vamot* 64a explains that a myriad is in fact 10,000 and 'according to the rule מיעוט רבים שנים "myriads" will denote [at least] two myriads (twenty thousands) and "thousands" will denote [at least] two thousand, giving 22,000.'[2]

According to *Torah* however, 600,000[3] Israelites left and Abraham was promised countless descendents.[4] *Sifre* thus brings quite a radical statement to explain why this relatively small number is used in our verse,

ובנחה יאמר וגו' מגיד הכתוב כשהיו ישראל נוסעים אלפים וחונים רבבות אמר משה איני מניח את השכינה עד שתעשה לישראל רבבות ואלפים שמתשובה שאמר אתה יודע מה אמר להם ה' אלהי אבותיכם [וגו'] יוסיף עליכם ככם אלף פעמים (דברים א') אמרו לו משה רבינו הרי אנו מובטחים לברכות הרבה ואתה נותן קצבה לברכותינו א"ל אני בשר ודם יש קצבה לברכותי זו משלי אבל הוא יברך אתכם כאשר דבר לכם כחול ימים וכצמחי אדמה וכדגי הים וככוכבי השמים (אבל) הוא יברך כאשר דבר להם לרוב

('And when it rested etc'. The verse teaches that Israel travelled in their thousands and encamped in their tens of

---

1. *Sifre Bamidbar B'ha'alotcha Piska* 26. In *Yalkut Shimoni* and the Maharal's *Chiddushey Aggudot* this statement is attributed to R. Dostai.
2. Silberman, *op. cit.*, p190. The plural number, רבבות (myriads) and אלפי (thousands) having been used in both cases. The plural signifies not less than two. (*Y'vamot* 64a Soncino *Talmud, op. cit.*, note e(8)).
3. See *Bamidbar* 1:46 (the exact figure given was 630,550).
4. See *B'reshit* 22:17 and 26:4.

thousands. Moses said[1] I am not going to let the Divine Presence rest until You make Israel [into] myriads of thousands. For from the answer that he gave, you know what he had said to them, 'May the Lord, God of your fathers ... add to you as them a thousandfold' (*D'varim* 1:11). They [the Israelites] said to Moses our teacher, behold we were promised a blessing of many [more] but you set a limit to our our blessing. He said, I am but flesh and blood and have a limit to my blessing, but He will bless you as he has spoken to you as the sands of the sea and the plants of the earth and the fish of the sea and the stars of the skies, He will bless you as he spoke you them to increase.)[2]

Moses (clearly not content with apparently ordering God to move - see earlier) is now telling God that He cannot even rest until Israel is fortified to the tune of 'myriads of thousands.' Moses reassures the Israelites that they will reach larger numbers but not yet, he is limiting things to mere thousands. But if this is the case, why do our commentators generally signify this as particularly meaning 22,000?

In his *Chiddushim* to *Y'vamot* 64a, the Maharasha[3] explains that the righteous are called "the Divine Chariot", and that this indeed was the number of the Levites the tribe who did not worship the Golden Calf, and who therefore were privileged

---

1. In *Yalkut Shimoni*, the text reads ... כביכול אמר משה (*as it were* Moses said ...), emphasising how radical this statement is and the need to preface it with 'as it were'.
2. *Sifre Bamidbar B'ha'alotcha Piska* 26.
3. Samuel Eliezer Edels c.1558-1631.
   כן בדוגמא זו היה באותו דור מחנה לויה כ"ב אלף כולם צדיקים שהשכינה שורה עליהם ... והם היו ממש המרכבה
   (And so in this example, in that same generation was the camp of Levi, 22,000, all righteous such that the *Shechinah* rested upon them... and they were in reality the [Divine] Chariot). The Maharal similarly explains that ולפיכך היו הלוים כ"ב אלף שהם מחנה השכינה (and that is why the Levites were 22,000, for they were the camp of the *Shechinah* (*Gur Aryeh Bamidbar amud* 49)).

that they should become 'the bearers of the God idea in Israel',[1] as well as the physical bearers of the Ark of the Covenant.[2]

Israel survived the Golden Calf incident through the merit of the Levites and the implication is that we are not therefore looking merely at 22,000 people but 22,000 **righteous and god-fearing** people out of the 600,000.

K'lei Yakar who posed the original question as to why if, even though it had no commandments therein, our 'book' was nonetheless still deemed important, employs this rationale to answer his own question,

אענה אני חלקי ואומר שלמצוות פריה ורביה עשה ספר בפני עצמו כי במצוה זו תלוי קיום העולם וגורם השראת השכינה כמ"ש רז"ל (יבמות סד) כל מי שאינו עוסק בפו"ר גורם לשכינה שתסתלק מישראל ... הרי שהיו ישראל כ"ב אלף פחות אחד וזה שלא עסק בפו"ר ... כך עשה ספר מיוחד ממצוה זו ... וממילא ידע כל איש מישראל להיות זהיר במצות פו"ר למלאות המספר ...

(I will answer, for my part and say [it is] for the commandment of 'be fruitful and multiply' it was made a book by itself, for the existence of the world is dependent on this commandment and a factor in the Divine Presence remaining [with us], as our Rabbis of blessed memory said (in *Y'vamot*), all who do not occupy themselves in 'be fruitful and multiply' cause the Divine Presence to depart from Israel ... if there were 22,000 less [even] one because they did not occupy themselves in themselves in 'be fruitful and multiply' ... thus He made a special book from this commandment ... so that each man from Israel will be careful in the commandment 'be fruitful and multiply' to ensure this number ...)

---

1. Silbermann, *op. cit.*, p190.
2. *Bamidbar* 3:35.

The argument here seems to be the simple expedient that the greater the number of Jews the greater the chances of finding 22,000 that are going to be righteous!

For the anonymous sage in *Y'vamot and K'lei Yakar* at least, the duty of פרו ורבו (be fruitful and multiply) is the way to ensure Jewish survival and we can see here a solution proffered by the ultra-orthodox community whose approach is to have many children and so preserve the heritage. *Y'vamot* 64a adds additional information, quoting a further biblical reference proving that the need for children is paramount,

להיות לך לאלהים ולזרעך אחריך בזמן שזרעך אחריך שכינה שורה אין זרעך אחריך על מי שורה על העצים ועל האבנים

('To be a God to you and to your seed after you' (*Bereshit* 17:7). Where there exists a seed after you the Divine Presence dwells amongst them but where no seed after you exists among whom shall it dwell? Amongst the trees or amongst the stones?)

This phrase almost suggests that by having children that come after you - and perhaps we could read אחריך *achareycha* as implying that they follow *after your ways* and embrace Judaism - we gain the merit of having God present with us and our own actions are not enough, we must act to continue Judaism through having offspring and our children too must be righteous.[1]

This has profound implications for a community that is often not tolerant of children in the synagogue and where many youth have opted out because the services contain no meaning

---

1. The Maharasha holds a similar view, stating,
   בזמן שזרעך אחריך כמותך צדיק השכינה שורה עליו ובזמן שאין לך זרע אחריך כמותך אלא שהוא רשע אין השכינה שורה עליו
   (In a time where your seed after you are like you, righteous, the *Shechinah* dwells upon him, but in a time where your seed is not after you, i.e. like you, rather he is evil, the *Shechinah* does not dwell upon him.)

for them. Congregations may invest heavily in education and youth but it is the duty of the home and family to inculcate strong Jewish values and practice. Moreover each and every child must be a valued as part of the community as any, for with the loss of even one of those *potential* righteous people, can cause the *Shechinah* to depart, for as *Bava Kama* states,

והיתה אשה מעוברת ביניהם וראויה להשלים ונבח בה כלב והפילה נמצא זה גורם לשכינה שתסתלק מישראל

(if there were among them [i.e. Israel] a pregnant woman capable of completing that number [i.e. the magical 22,000], but a dog barked and she miscarried, the dog would, in this case, have caused the *Shechinah* to depart from Israel.)

Iturei Torah[1] also takes this section together with the previous verse as indicating recognition of the need to preserve the Jewish people. His interpretation not only lends the importance to the book and also gives it a timeless quality making it applicable to all generations - or indeed all the 'myriads and families of Israel'.

He states,

החשיבות על שום מה כי בפסוקים האלא ... מקופלת כל ההיסטוריה שלנו ויהי בנסע בשעת צרה נדודים גירושים וגלות שסכנה שהאויב יעשה בנו כלה על כך התפלל משה קומה ה' ויפוצו אויבך וכו' ובנחה בשעת מרגוע צפויה סכנה של טמיעה ושל התבוללות והתכחשות לה' לעמו ולתורתו על כך התפלל משה שובה ה' רבבות אלפי ישראל השב כל האלפים של ישראל למקום במספרם

(Why is it important? Because in these [two] verses 'and when the Ark set off', 'and when it rested' unfolds all our history. 'And when the Ark set off' [indicating that] in a time of trouble, floggings, [forced] conversions and exile, [and] that of the perils that the enemy will do against all of us. Because of this, Moses prayed 'Arise O Lord and scatter your

---

1. By Rabbi Aharon Ya'akov Greenberg Aharon.

enemies ...' 'And when it rested' - at a time of tranquility[1] [i.e. relative peace for the community]; foreseeing the danger of assimilation and of merging and of denying of God and His people and His Law, Moses prayed 'Return O Lord; the myriads of the families of Israel' [which should be read as] return all the families and the myriads of Israel to the places in their numbers [i.e. that there be none lacking].)

We can thus see in our verses the twin duties of survival in times of hardship - ensuring we don't buckle before the oppressor and abandon our faith, but, more relevant to us in our relative security, the restatement of the objectives of continuity, the duty of preventing the assimilation of ourselves and our youngsters.

Thus every person lost to Judaism by not raising their children Jewishly or through their own assimilation, potentially depletes the chances of finding 22,000 righteous souls and eats away at heart of the *Schechinah*.

Simply put, this section of *Sefer Binsoa* teaches us that if we don't PROTECT our Judaism, we won't SURVIVE.

---

1. Rashi similarly notes in his commentary to verse 36, ובה ה' מנחם תרגמו לשון מרגוע ('Return Lord', Menachem in his translation, [explains this as the] language of tranquility).

CHAPTER 4

But our job here is not finished there. It is not enough to see to our own and our own descendents survival Jewishly. We have a greater mission.

Ibn Ezra notes that God is requested to arise,[1] כדי בני אדם לעמוד להלחם (as a man stands to do battle) and whilst this may be less than palatable to modern ears, it is on this more militaristic approach to the text that we will now dwell. Fohrer views our verses as 'a formula and saying of everyday life ... [for] particularly in the pre-monarchic period, when there was no standing army of professional soldiers, the conduct of war could be associated with religious ideas and customs, which are connected with attempts to gain victory and avoid defeat by means of divine aid.'[2]

Anderson too recognises this as 'one of the oldest fragments of the Pentateuch' referring to it as 'the "Song of the Ark"', again as if it was a set phrase for use in a military situation -

---

1. Milgrom notes that 'the verb *kam* signifies advancing or rising in order to attack (c.f. Judges 5:12) and the noun *kam* means attacker (Exod. 15:7)'. Milgrom, J, *op. cit.*, p81.
2. Fohrer G, *Introduction to the Old Testament*, Abigdon Press, 1968.

almost as a protective charm.[1]

Indeed, Moses, expression רבבות אלפי can be translated as 'the countless armed units'; *Aleph* being the smallest military division, and this narrows the scope of Moses' request for protection considerably with him asking God only to return the fighters safely from battle, not all of Israel.[2] Alternatively the phrase could be translated as You who are the myriads of thousands; 'in other words ... God ... is declared equivalent to [the] hordes of His armies, in a similar way.'[3]

This all seems to be a request for, or statement of, a positive nature requesting victory, and yet we are informed by the Sages that any verse that begins ויהי *vay'hi* (and it was) actually 'alludes to sadness'[4] and claims *Tiferet Yonatan*, this verse is no exception.

Sforno doesn't mention specifically the two sins we have already spoken off, but explains that the damning report of the spies and the people's despondency was the reason for the failure of Moses' prayer to come to pass, for,

---

1. Anderson, B W, *The Living World of the Old Testament*, Longman 1988, p117. Alter notes that 'there is sufficient evidence of poetic structure and diction even in the brief fragment. Rhythmically these two verses contain, respectively, three of four stresses, a pattern sometimes found in Biblical poetry. The word pairings, enemies/foes, scatter/flee, are a hallmark of parallelistic poetry.' He also notes that '"Rise" as several commentators have noted, also has a military sense of "attack"' (Alter, R, *The Five Books of Moses*, W. W. Norton & Company, NY, 2004, p73).
2. Milgrom, J, *op. cit.*, p81.
3. *Ibid.*
4. *Hamaayan*, The Torah Spring Vol 10 No.32, ed. Katz, S, published on the internet 1996. *M'gillah* 10b explains that,

   זה מסורת בידינו מאנשי כנסת הגדולה כל מקום שנאמר ויהי אינו אלא לשון צער

   (it is a tradition that comes to us from the men of the great assembly that in all places it says 'and it came to pass' it indicates [the approach] of trouble') and goes on to list various examples, though not our verse.

כי אמנם לולא שלחו מרגלים היו נכנסים בזולת מלחמה שהיו האומות בורחים ...

(had they not sent the spies they would have entered [Israel] without [recourse to] war, for the nations would have fled ...) and for him our verses are not misplaced but 'follow logically in sequence ... since the Israelites were about to enter the Promised Land ... [and] that it would not have been necessary for Israel to wage war since the Almighty Himself would have driven out the nations from Canaan.'[1]

Solveitchik, who likewise dwells on the military angle, also notes that what we have in these two verses is a reminder of a campaign that failed to live up to expectations. Because of the various failings of the Israelites - their murmuring, Miriam's sin and subsequent leprosy and the 'unfortunate episode of *Vayikhu Ha'am balayla hazeh* (and the people cried the entire night of *Tisha B'av* after the return of the spies)' - the original plan that God would scatter the enemies and cause them to flee allowing the Israelites to 'conquer the land without so much as a battle' was voided and instead the Israelites under Joshua would have seven years of battle. For Soloveitchik, our two verses aren't the book entire, instead they 'would have been the first and last verses of an additional book of the Torah ... and between [them] would have told the complete story of how the conquest of the Land by *Moshe* and *B'nay Yisrael* [for] had *Moshe* entered the land we would have merited seeing the fulfilment of *Kumah Hashem Vyafutsu Oyvecha* ... and the conquest of the land would have been immediate.'[2]

Our two verses thus, for Slolveitchik at least, represent a '*Sefer Shalem*, a <u>potential</u> complete book of the Torah'[3] that

---

1. Pelcovitz, *op. cit.*, p697.
2. *Shiur* HaRav Soloveitchik on *Parshas Bha'aloscha* (6/7/77), summarised by Dr. I Rivik and J Rapps and published on the internet 1997.
3. *Ibid.*

was not actually fulfilled and are encased in the *nunim hafuchim* for this reason.

Similarly Hirsch's translation and commentary on the parallel text in *T'hillim* 68:2, יקום אלוקים יפוצו אויביו reads, '<u>were</u> God to arise, His enemies would be scattered ...' instead of the more literal translation, 'God will arise ...' Hirsch explains that 'if God were to rise up in all His might, [then] all the wicked of the Earth would perish immediately.'[1] God, however, does not and did not meet fully the expectations of this verse for 'had Israel already reached the heights which a true realisation of the Lawgiving on the Mount of God assumes, the further course of its history would have taken a different and simpler path. The way from the Mount of God would have led immediately to the Land of God.'[2]

Me'am Lo'ez provides yet another explanation for the two inverted *nuns* and why the letter *nun* in particular was chosen which also echoes this sense of the failure of the Israelites to capitalise on the opportunity that the occasion offered. It explains that 'the great merit of the the Israelites ... stemmed from [their having uttered] two words at Mount Sinai: *na'aseh* (נעשה) "we shall do" and *nishma* (נשמע)[3] "we shall heed."[4] We further learn that 'when God appeared on the mountain of Sinai, he was accompanied by 600,000 angelic beings that bestowed upon every Israelite two crowns, bearing the inscription of God's Explicit Name. These corresponded to *Na'aseh* (נעשה) and *nishma* (נשמע). At this time, they were more beloved than angels, having become transformed into spiritual beings.'[5]

---

1. Hirsch, S R, *The Psalms*, Feldheim Publishers, Jerusalem/New York 1978, p454.
2. Hirsch, S R, *The Pentatuech - Bamidbar, op. cit.*, p1145.
3. *Sh'mot* 24:7.
4. *Yalkut Me'am Lo'ez on Bamidbar*, Moznaim Publishing Corporation, 1990, p278.
5. *Ibid.*

But such faith is sadly not to last and instead now 'they were determined to free themselves of the yoke [of self-control] imposed upon them by the Torah, and were running away from Mount Sinai, like a man running away from a conflagration. So correspondingly the Nun's were overturned, symbolizing the fact that now their condition was the obverse of what it had been when they exclaimed "We shall do, and we shall heed (נעשה ונשמע). In this connection, note that the name of the Hebrew letter Nun (נ'ו'ן) is the acrostic of *na'aseh v'nishma* (נ'עשה ו' נ'שמע).'[1]

Ittur Bikurim[2] similarly notes that 'this explains why the letters *nun* are reversed: in order to indicate that the Israelites deviated from the proper path and sinned, the letters are not inscribed in their proper manner.'

This 'bad news' is compounded, according to *Tiferet Yonatan*,[3] who explains that the proceeding verse reports that the Ark travelled three days ahead but 'had [it] travelled among *B'nei Yisrael*, it would have destroyed them when they rebelled.'[4]

But what is this wasted opportunity for victory? Is it simply the conquest of the Land or is it something greater?

Continuing on the military theme, we can now turn our attention to the enemy, *Sifre* notes,

וינוסו משנאיך וכי יש שונאים לפני מי שאמר והיה העולם אלא מגיד הכתוב שכל מי ששונא את ישראל כמי ששונא את המקום

---

1. *Ibid.*
2. Rav Shmuel Avigdor Bar Avraham Tosfaa, Vilna 1837.
3. Jonathan Eybeschutz, born in Krakow 1690, died in Altona 1764.
4. *Hamaayan, op. cit.* However Rambam and Abravanel translate this as 'on that three days journey' as if it were 'a distance of three days' then it would have not been 'visible in order to serve as a guide' (Milgrom, J, *op. cit.*, p80).

('and cause your enemies to flee' - and who can hate He who spoke and the world existed. Rather the verse teaches us that all who hate Israel it is as if they hate the Omnipresent.)[1]

Sifre asks who can possibly be, and more importantly remain, an enemy of the omnipotent God, and answers that these are those that hate Israel and all that it stands for. God and by implication us, as His allies, are to scatter these individuals.

Rashi's comments to the parallel text in *T'hillim* 68:2 tells us that יקום אלקים יפוצו אויביו עמלק וכיוצא בו ('God will arise and scatter His foes' - these are *Amalek* and those like him).

Israel's traditional military enemy is thus revealed. However, are we to continue to read this purely in the militarist vein of the historical perspective of the conquest of the land? Or, can we perceive some deeper meaning. As we have seen, God if He so wished could have very easily scatter the foe, but Hirsch suggests that 'The Lord, however employs other means to bring about the advent of his kingdom on earth.'[2]

Hirsch also explains that, 'Moses recognized that this Torah from its very entry into the world would have to expect enemies, opponents, and foes, that people would hate it. Its demands for justice and love are so very much in opposition to the dictates of force and selfishness, the curse of which is felt so keenly by the weak and needy. Those in power unite in an alliance to impose these dictates. They are the enemies of the Torah who form a tacitly united front, opponents of the Torah who bar the entry of its influence into the world. Its demands for self-control and sanctification of morals are so much in conflict with the allures of ignoble passion that one finds among all classes not only those who oppose it but also

---

1. *Sifre Bamidbar B'ha'alotcha Piska* 26.
2. Hirsch, S R, *The Psalms, op. cit.*, p454.

those who incite against it, not only hate but also persecution ...'[1]

החפץ אחפץ מות רשע נאם אדני יהוה הלוא בשובו מדרכיו וחיה
(Have I any pleasure at all that the wicked should die? says the Lord God; and not rather that he should return from his ways, and live?)[2] writes the prophet *Yechezkiel* explaining that not the sinner but the sin must die, and perhaps similarly here we are talking about the foe being scattered and fleeing, perhaps it is not the actual physical enemy but the non-Jewish values and ideals that they stand for. The corruption, greed and materialistic desires and injustices that are all to commonplace in the world. Certainly Hertz explains *'rise up O Lord ... before thee* [is] the impressive victory war cry of truth against error, of righteousness against sin.'[3]

We have already mentioned that some consider these two verses as a *t'filat haderech* (wayfarers prayer) and indeed the *Emek HaMelech*[4] explains that 'whoever reads this chapter daily with proper intention will not be hurt, even when he may travel to a place of thieves, at sea or in another dangerous location.' The enemies here are not just people but rather the very real dangers that inhabit the world and could beset the innocent and law-abiding Jew.

As Simon Jacobson explains 'despite life's hardships, we do not come unarmed. The Holy Ark leads the way, and in its wake 'enemies' are scattered and 'foes' flee. The Torah - called 'Torah of life' and the 'Torah of light' - illuminates the dark and lonely paths of existence and empowers us with direction, fortitude and commitment to make it through the

---

1. Hirsch S R, *Bamidbar op. cit.*
2. *Y'chezkiel* 18:23.
3. Hertz, J H, *Daily Prayer Book*, Shapiro Vallentine and Co., London 1955, p474.
4. Gate I section 59. Written by 17th century Kabbalist, Rabbi Naftali Hertz Bachrach of Frankfurt.

most challenging experiences of life.'[1] Similarly the *Chabad Rebbe* Menachem M. Schneerson explains that the Ark was carried along with a container of Manna and that when we take out the *Torah*, representing the Ark that 'God ... blesses us that we should earn a living comfortably, enabling the *mitsvos* to be performed free from worry and concern.'[2]

Alternatively this prayer by Moses represents not protection from the physical foes or even physical danger or need, but instead could be a spiritual battleground and the enemy of Israel and God is in fact within each Israelite him or herself. We would therefore be requesting from God assistance in scattering, defeating or at least containing our *yetser ha-ra* (evil inclination). *D'varim* 23:10 reads,

כי תצא מחנה על איביך ונשמרת מכל דבר רע (When the camp goes out against your enemies, then you shalt guard yourself from every evil thing.)

As well as our physical enemies directly referred to, this also infers the need to rise up and fight against our lesser nature, our animal soul represented by the *yetser ha-ra*. Here prayer itself is the weapon and our voices and our petitions to God allow us to combat something we would otherwise have little control over. It is only with God's help that we can best our desires and similarly in our verses, Moshe thus could well call upon God to rise up and scatter the spiritual foe of our own darker natures as we would be unable to do this on our own.[3]

Hertz concurs and explains that 'a community, like and

---

1. Jacobson S, *Beha'alotcha: A Secret Formula for Protection*, OP-ED Weekly 2009.
2. *The Gutnick Edition Chumash*, Miller C, *Kol Menachem*, 2009, p927. Based on *Sefer Hasichos* 5751 vol. 1 p381 and note 24 *ibid*. A clear example here of the recognition of Maslow's hierarchy of needs that spiritual goals are much harder to attain if simple basic necessities are not catered for.
3. I'm grateful for a *d'var torah* by R. Y. Alperowitz of *Chabad* Bournemouth for allowing me to make this connection to our verses.

individual is unable to emerge from religious apathy my mere fiat of will alone. "No prisoner can by himself free himself from prison" say the Rabbis.[1] People have to have 'the desire for the life illumined and transformed by Religion'[2] and then God will come to their aid.

Schneerson notes that just as we take out the Torah from the Ark to these verses, this 'is the moment when God actually instills his people with the spirit of resilience and dedication required to 'take out' the values of Torah and apply them to ones every day life'[3] and that may your foes be scattered' refers to the 'the withdrawal from things that are counter productive to a Torah lifestyle.'[4] This all sits well with the later references to *t'shuvah* (repentance) alluded to in verse 36.[5]

Like *Iturei Torah*, Hirsch too believes that these two verses 'comprise a compendium of the whole history of Israel.'[6] However unlike the explanation above which proposed a defensive retention of our Jewish identity in the face of adversity in a reactive manner, Hirsch's ideas represent a far more pro-active stance where the Ark's movement represents Judaism as is carried into the world. For Hirsch, Moses had already recognised the there would be opponents to the *Torah* moving into the world which would result in persecution of the bearers of the God idea, however, the command 'arise' speaks not only to God as a protector of the people, but also to us, stressing that we should also arise positively promote Judaism as through such actions 'its [i.e. *Torah*'s] penetrating entry would make the coalition of its enemies disperse and the persecuting hate take to flight before it.'[7]

---

1. Hertz, J H, *Daily Prayer Book, op. cit.*
2. *Ibid.*
3. *The Gutnick Chumash, op. cit.*, p927.
4. *Ibid.*
5. See chapter 5.
6. Hirsch S R, *Bamidbar op. cit.*
7. *Ibid.* The Artscroll *siddur* similarly comments on our verses that 'by

These ideas go far beyond the mere preservation of Judaism alluded to above or our own self-improvement through the *mitsvot* that God gives us to defeat our evil inclination. Here we have an oblique reference to the 'divine mission' to bring God and the ideals of Judaism to the whole of mankind. This is a much more positive image than Ibn Ezra's 'man of war'.

Another meaning of the root פוץ is 'break through'[1] and instead of physically scattering, the people Israel is assisting God in the 'breaking through' of the ideas of ethical monotheism and the promotion of distinctly Jewish values to others.

These ideas have been crystalised over time as Israel's task to be a 'light unto the nations.'[2] And indeed this is something we often forget. Lord Jacobowitz noted that 'we have become altogether to inward looking, with our horizons largely linked within the ghetto-walls we have erected to separate us from the rest of our people and from the human society beyond ... preoccupied with the burning problems of our own survival, we have lost sight of our assignment as a light unto the nations.'[3] Perhaps we shouldn't have, as his successor Chief Rabbi Sacks notes 'though we loved humanity, we have never stopped wrestling with it and challenging the idols of every age.'[4] It is simply our job.

Being a 'light unto the nations', however, generally accepted

---

blessing [God] for having given us the Torah, we accept our responsibility to carry out its commands and **spread its message'**. *The Complete Artscroll Siddur*, Mesorah Publications Ltd., 1984, p433.

1. Jastrow, M, *op. cit.*
2. ונתתיך לאור גוים להיות ישועתי עד־קצה הארץ (I will give you as a light unto the nations, that My salvation may be to the end of the earth (*Yeshayah* 49:6).)
3. Jacobowitz, I, *The Timely and the Timeless*, Vallentine Mitchell, London 1977), p96-97.
4. Sacks, J, *Ten Days Ten Ways - Paths to Divine Presence*, US Office of the Chief Rabbi, 2009, p60.

to be Israel setting an example of fine and Godly behaviour rather than any pro-active 'attack' on other ways, secular or religious.

Judaism today and for many centuries has not been seen as a proselytising religion and indeed certain sections of our community actively discourage this.[1] However Hirsch notes that the reference to רבבות אלפי ישראל does not refer to Moses' own time, rather it is 'the myriads that would ensue from the thousands of Jews, by descending from them and by **attachment** to them.'[2] We have already considered the over-riding need for our descendants who adhere to the faith, but the last idea is worthy of exploration as it suggests that גרים *gerim* (proselytes) should also be included in these myriads and that we should perhaps be more active in encouraging the growth of the community by this means as well as spreading Jewish messages amongst the wider community effectively 'scattering' other ideals. This is perhaps supported by reference to a verse from the traditional passage that serves as *haftorah* for *B'ha'alotcha* where we find,

ונלוו גוים רבים אל ה' ביום ההוא והיו לי לעם ושכנתי בתוכך וידעת כי ה' צבאות שלחני אליך

(And many nations will attach themselves unto God on that day and will become My people and I will dwell in your midst).[3]

Z'chariah, is here suggesting 'the possibility of actively converting gentiles. The expression "become My people" was probably unsettling for many of his listeners',[4] as it is to many of us today. However, perhaps he considered this a

---

1. Recent developments have taken the discouragement of proselytes to a new level and have even worryingly introduced the concept of retrospectively making *pasul* past conversions.
2. Hirsch S R, *Bamidbar op. cit.*
3. *Z'chariah* 2:15.
4. Plaut G W & Stern C, *The Haftarah Commentary, op. cit.*, p348.

missed opportunity and something for which Jews should be actively struggling; for unlike what is written of the Israelites when they were rebelling; that the *Shechinah* was three days away from them, once the mission has been fulfilled through spreading Jewish ideals and drawing the non-Jew near to God, ושכנתי בתוכך (My *Shechinah* will dwell amongst you).[1]

Linking this back to Soloveitchik and Hirsch's ideas that the purpose of the 'book' and thus creation is not fulfilled, it is perhaps possible that Israel may have entered the land, but that the delay meant that all was not right and the mission remained uncompleted. This could in turn be the reason for the use of יקום ('He **will** arise' (*T'hillim* 68:2)) and יאמר ('[Moses] **will** say' (*Bamidbar* 10:36).)

The victory is perhaps as much a spiritual one as a physical inhabiting of the Land. We 'scatter' our own evil inclination and those things that seek to harm us by adhering to and trusting in God and His *Torah*. In doing so, we gain the strength of purpose to 'break through' the mundane idolatrous world bringing it the clear benefits of ethical monotheism, re-igniting our role as a 'light unto the nations' and hopefully drawing others to Judaism.

However, Moses is not yet able to allow God to 'rest' and God has not yet enabled Israel to scatter the foe. The process is still continuing. The Ark has not yet come to rest and God has not fully returned, but, says *Sefer Binsoa*, don't fear - these things **will** happen.

---

1. *Z'chariah* 2:15.

Chapter 5

We noted at the end of the last chapter that there is a sense of the unfinished, the incomplete within the two verses, which is reflected by its possible mis-positioning. Yet there are two words in our text that require further investigation as they convey a hope that things can indeed be made whole.

The use of the word שובה *shuvah* (return) is too great a temptation for the rabbis to resist linking our verse with the concept of תשובה *t'shuvah* (repentance) and applying it not to God but instead to Israel. Ibn Ezra explains that,

שובה ה' אמר רבי יהודה המדקדק הראשון כי כל שב שטעמו מגזרת תשובה הוא פועל עומד ולא יוצא בבנין הקל רק אם היה טעמו בשלוה והשקט כמו בשובה ונחת תושעון כן שובה ה' רבבות אלפי ישראל שניחם ולא ירגזו מאויב ... ומשה התפלל שניח וישקיט השם כל ישראל ואם הם רבים

('Return Lord', Rabbi Yehuda, the first grammarian said that in every place we find [the root] *shuv*, its reason is to indicate repentance, it is an active verb and not transitive in a simple form, only if its reason [was to indicate] tranquility and quiet as in calm and rest thus 'return Hashem the myriads of thousands of Israel' who are at rest and not agitated by the enemy ... and Moshe prayed for God to put at ease and quieten all Israel, even if they are many.)

Rashi explains,

שובה ה' מנחם תרגמו לשון מרגוע וכן [ישעיה ל] בשובה ונחת תושעון

(Menachem translates - this is the language of rest/calm and such [is found in *Y'shayah* 30:15] 'in sitting still and rest shall ye be saved'.)[1]

So here we see an equating of the idea of repentance with that of peace and quiet of mind as well as surroundings. If we repent, then perhaps this our reward. Certainly the reverse holds true - that if we know we have done wrong and we do not repent then we will have a sense of unease, that something remains undone and that will sit upon our shoulder nagging at us to do something about it and put our life back into balance.

It is up to us to make restitution for our past behaviours so that we can both return and rest, but, as we learnt earlier we cannot conquer our evil inclination without the help of God and so we have also seen above that God is 'not allowed' by Moses to rest until His promises to us are fulfilled and he assists us.

What does it mean for God to rest? We learn that God rested on the seventh day and made it holy and the *Shabbat* was made for man to give him a fore-taste of the world to come, a

---

1. *Y'shayah* 30:15 reads,

    כי כה אמר אדני יהוה קדוש ישראל בשובה ונחת תושעון בהשקט ובבטחה תהיה גבורתכם ...

    (For thus said the Lord God, the Holy One of Israel: in sitting still and rest shall you be saved, in quietness and in confidence shall be your strength ...)

sense of completeness.[1] As we become complete through repentance so it makes, *kivyachol*, God complete. For even though God is infinite and we are nothing and the whole universe has little effect on Him, yet we all have the spark of the Divine and as we correct ourselves we help God's more immanent presence become complete through our personal *tikkun* (repair).

We have already made reference to that immanent presence, the *Shechinah*, and at its simplest, it is the use of ובנוחה with it's feminine ending[2] that perhaps signifies that it is the *Shechinah* that will return not just the Ark. Certainly this is a common connection made in the midrashic texts.

In the *Zohar*, Rabbi El'azar[3] seems to have a a much more positive view than *Me'am Loez* about the reason for the letters facing backwards. It isn't that the Jews were abandoning the concept of נעשה ונשמע (we will do and [then] we will hear.)[4]

Instead,

נ לא הוה מתפרש מניה ונטיל עמיה ומגו רחימו דלהון דישראל אהדר אנפוי ואסתחר מלפני ארונא ... וע"ד בנסוע הארון נו"ן אחסר אנפין לקבלייהו דישראל וכתבי גופא לגבי ארונא

(the *nun* represents the *Shechinah* who was travelling along and did not leave. Due to their love for Israel, He [God]

---

1. The word for peace - *shalom* is related to *shalem* (wholeness).
2. This is the *K'tiv* (written form). The *K'ri* (verbalised form) is the expected masculine ובנוחו. Ibn Ezra focuses on the fact that instead of it being written with a *vav*, *u'v'nucho* ends with a *heh*. But discounts this as having any meaning by suggesting that (the letters *aleph, heh, vav* and *yud* are [basically] interchangeable). Indeed these are the letters that often are different as their absence or presence doesn't always change the meaning of the word. However, others tend to suggest that usually such a change signifies some hidden meaning.
3. 5th generation *Tanna*, son of Rabbi Shim'on bar Yochai who is traditionally regarded as the author of the *Zohar*.
4. See chapter 4.

turned His face back to Israel, and She [the Shechinah] turned herself around from the Ark ... therefore, when the Ark set forth, the nun turned her face back towards the children of Israel and the shoulders of her body towards the Ark.)

Indeed the text also explains that even though Israel,

מארח מישר קודשא בריך הוא לא בעי לשבקא לון ובכל זמנא אהדר אנפוי לקבלייהו דאי לאו הכי לא יקומון בעלמא

(diverged from the straight path [through their complaints] the Holy One Blessed be He did not forsake them. He always turns His face back towards them, for had it not been so, they would never have been able to survive in the world.)[1]

Commenting on the shape of the *nun hafucha*, *Lishkat Hasofer*[2] explains that,

וצרתן כזה היינו ראש כדרכה ורגלה כפוף לאחרי' כאדם הכורע על ברכיו

(and its form is like this - its head as its [normal] way but its leg bent behind it like a man who is upon kneeling upon his knees)[3] and as well as further reinforcing the 'S' or 'Z' shape we have seen earlier,[4] the image conjured up is one of the penitent on his knees praying before God for forgiveness.

However it is worth noting that only after the Ark was actually at rest did Moses invoke the idea of repentance. The

---

1. In this section from the *Zohar*, Rabbi Shim'on bar Yochai and his son Rabbi El'azar have a brief and complex argument about whether and when *Malchut* (the divine emanation of Kinship, one of the ten *sefirot*) symbolised by the letter *nun* was withdrawn from Israel and put into exile as punishment by means of God turning his face away. Rabbi El'azar maintains that, '*Malchut* did not turn her face away from the children of Israel meaning that it did not cease its influence.' Rabbi Shim'on however sees this negatively and instead references that, 'after the Ark came to rest the people complained and they caused *Malchut* to turn her back on them.'
2. Ganzfreid's own commentary on his work *Keset Hasofer*.
3. We saw a similar view from the Recanti. See introduction.
4. See introduction.

sequence here is clear, unlike the first verse where we are unsure of whether the Ark moves and then the invocation was made or vice versa. Here God decides when to rest and needs to be entreated to return to Israel.

Indeed Sforno recognises the need to ensure God is still with the people, despite also being out conquering the enemy,
שובה תהי מנוחתך פה עמנו כענין זאת מנוחתי עדי עד ואף על פי שתגלה שכינתך לפני ישראל לגרש את אויביהם תהי מנוחת שכינתך בתוכנו

('Return' - let your rest be here amongst us, in this matter, this is my rest for ever and even if you send out Your *Shechinah* (Divine Presence) before Israel to drive away their enemies, let the resting of Your *Shechinah* be amongst us.)

This implies that there can be no return/repentance without rest first. Perhaps if we are too tired or troubled and have no place where we can have quiet enough to examine our own soul through prayer, then we cannot truly repent. Perhaps peace and tranquility are not just the reward but in fact are pre-requisites for proper repentance. You need to take time out for contemplation. If something is troubling you, then you can't focus on your own self-repair.

Sometimes the silent prayer of the individual may be what is required rather than the noise of communal prayer. At other times it may be that the backdrop of the spiritual energy of a community at prayer which provides the channel by which we can suddenly lose ourselves in the *kavannah* (spiritual intention) that would allow us a clear direct link to God.

The message, however, is clear - Israel is only guaranteed divine protection when it is free from sinning and has thrown off the evil inclination (in this specific case manifested by the constant Israelite complaints against God). Since none of us are free from sin, this makes the concept of prayer leading to repentance that sits within the root of returning all the more important. God will return to us if we are serious about returning to him.[1]

We have already seen that 'the number upon which the *Shechinah* rests is 22,000 ... because *Hashem* does not rest His presence on individual things, only on "complete" things'[2] and the Maharal in his *Chidushey Aggadot* explains what is so complete and perfect about our verses,

אין השכינה שורה כו' פי' דבר זה לפי דעתי כי התחלת הכל הוא התורה שהתורה נבראת תחלה והתחלת התורה היא כ"ב אותיות דהיינו אלפא ביתא וידוע כי השם יתברך מצטרף ביותר אל התחלה וכאשר הם ישראל כ"ב אלף כנגד כ"ב אותיות שהם התחלת התורה ואז הש"י מתחבר להם ושורה שכינה בישראל

(The *Shechinah* does not rest ... in my opinion this means that the beginning of everything is the *Torah*, since the *Torah* was created first and the origination of *Torah* is 22 letters that we have as our alphabet it is known that that *Hashem*, may He be blessed, is joined most to the beginning, and when Israel are 22,000 as per the 22 letters that are the beginning of the *Torah*, then *Hashem*, may He be blessed, is joined to them and the *Shechinah* is alongside Israel.)

This is a key concept too, signifying that perhaps the mere numbers of people involved - the 22,000 - isn't enough. Instead the people need to be joined to the idea of *Torah*, united and facing in one direction towards God - all of Israel are in it together. Indeed the Soncino Chumash,[3] translates 'ten thousands of the <u>families</u> of Israel'. Now, not all families are as united as they should be but again it suggests that we should all have the same aim. *Ba'al HaTurim* also notes that we have to work together in his exegesis of the word ובנחה noting the *k'ri-k'tiv*,

---

1. See the *midrash* from *Pesichta Rabbati* on page 43.
2. *Hamaayan, op. cit.*
3. *Soncino Chumash - The 5 Books of Moses with Haftarot,* Ed. Cohen, A, Soncino Press, 1990, p.843.

כתיב בה"א כנגד ארבעה דגלים ומחנה לויה (that it is spelt with a *heh* corresponding to the four divisions if the [Israelite] camp and the Levites.) As the Rokeach says, the word can be read as two words ובנח ה (at the resting of the five), i.e. the five camps.[1] The deliberate 'mis-spelling' is an allusion to the whole camp, the whole family of Israel having to return and rest as one.

A similar idea occurs with another *k'ri-k'tiv* in *Sh'mot* 19:2 and *Esther* 9:23 where the plural form *kiblu* (they accepted) is missing a *vav*. This oddity intimates that when at the foot of Mount Sinai our ancestors were 'as one man with one heart ... [and] after the miracle of Purim, our forefathers accepted the Torah a second time, and attained a similar 'one-ness'.'[2]

In our days of community strife and divisions between various factions symbolised by differing levels of observance and approaches to *halacha*, it is perhaps even more telling that the message of *Sefer Binsoa* is that the **whole** camp of Israel needs to draw together to merit God returning to them.

It is equally telling that we all have to affect some level of repentance and acceptance of God's will of their own accord. It is no surprise that tradition has in that *Mashiach* will only come when all Jews will keep a *Shabbat*, when all Jews are pointing towards the same goal and not 'in-fighting'.

As well as representing the whole of Jewish history as it effects the whole community - the 'family' of Israel - these two *p'sukim* reflect the realities of our daily life in our own immediate family and surroundings.

The core verbs in the first verse are very active נסע

---

1. *Ba'al Haturim Chumash - Bamidbar*, op. cit., p1476.
2. *The Wisdom of the Hebrew Alphabet*, Munk M, Mesorah Publications, 1995, p102.

(travelling) and קוּם (arise) - we get up in the morning, travel into our place of work and try to earn a living, try to do some good, make the world a better place, and perhaps 'scatter' some bad things pushing them away. But by evening, we are tired and we שוב (return) home, needing a well earned נוח (rest), we crash on the sofa with a nice cup of tea surrounded by the love of our family and protection of our home (our miniature sanctuary as much as any Synagogue is a miniature version of the Temple).

Similarly God decided to arise and set out to protect Israel and after the days travels and travails is asked to return to His family Israel *kivyachol* for some 'time out' with those who love Him - us.

CONCLUSION

Is *Sefer Binsoa* therefore **an important book**?

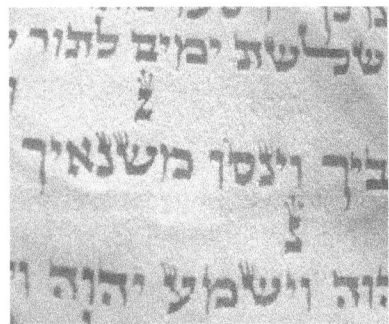

It is true that these two short *p'sukim* encased in their special signs appear not to contain any apparently new commandments, but they are, in their own way, a self contained history of the **purpose** of the Jewish nation.

These two *p'sukim* teach us that we need to be be so 'in tune' with the Almighty that His will and our will are interchangeable; that we are submitting to His will as if it were our own.

If we do this then we, like the Ark, are able to 'move forward', in that we become beloved partners of God and take the God-idea out into the world. We can confidently pass it on to our descendants and any others who may wish to join alongside us.

With such *bitachon* - trust, faith and confidence - we are better able to 'scatter' both the evil inclination that works within us and the the idolatrous ideas that we encounter all around us. Instead, we can set an example to the other nations of the world that a spiritual faith based approach to life is better than materialistic greed and any other modern idol that people 'worship'.

We will no doubt make mistakes - no one is perfect - but as long as through supplication and prayer we repent and return to God, then God will repay us by returning to us and protecting us from both the 'enemies' of physical and spiritual harm and by rewarding us with peace of mind and a sense of completeness.

He will then fully return to us and rest His Divine Presence upon us and bring the Messianic age speedily and in our days.

אמן כן יהי רצון

Bibliography

Hebrew sources:

B'ney Yonah/Uri Or, Landsofer Y, 1802.
Likut Sifrey STa"M I, (incorporating Keset Hasofer, Lishkat Hasofer, Alpha Beta, Shoneh Halachot, Kol Sofrim, Mishnat Sofrim, Tikkun T'fillin-Baruch She'amar, Da'at K'doshim (L'vush, Mikdash Me'at), Collected by R. T. Kohuna.
Likut Sifrey STa"M II, (incorporating D'varim Shebichtav, Kol Haremez, Kiryat Sefer, Lishkat Hasofer).
Melechat Shamayim, Bamberger Y, 1985.
Mikra'ot G'dolot, Pardes, 1951.
Mishnat Avraham, Avraham b. Zvi Yaffo, 1830.
Mishnah - Pirkey Avot.
Mishnat Hasofer al Hilchot STa"M, Yaakov Meir Stern, B'nei Brak, 1987.
Rambam Mishneh Torah: Hilchot T'fillin, Hilchot M'zuzah, Hilchot Sefer Torah.
Sifre with the commentary Emek HaN'tsiv, Jerusalem, (also includes emendations of the Vilna Gaon).
Torah Sh'lemah, Kasher, M M & Razhabi Yitshak, Leviticus Vol. 29, American Biblical Encyclopedia Society Inc., Jerusalem 1978.
Ot Y'ysiv - Hilchot STa"M, Hilberstam, Y, 2010.
Yalkut Tsurat Ha'Otiyot (incorporating 70 halachic texts on the formation of the letters), collected by David Lieb Greenfeld and Shmuel Eliyahu Granatstein, *Vaad Mishmeret STA"M*, Brooklyn, 1983.
Zohar.

English sources:

Alter, R, *The Five Books of Moses*, W. W. Norton & Company, NY, 2004.
Anderson, B, *The Living World of the Old Testament*, Longman 1998.
Ba'al Haturim Chumash-Bamidbar, R.Avie Gold, R. Eliyahu Touger, Mesorah Publications Ltd., 1999/2000.
Barthel, M, *What the Bible Really Says*, Wings Books, 1992.

Ed. Cohen A, *The Five Megilloth*, Soncino Press, London, 1975.
Ed. Cohen, A, *The Soncino Chumash*, The Soncino Press, NY, 1983.
Gershon, A G, *The Weekly Torah*, Chabad in Cyberspace 1996.
Ginsburg, C. D., *Introduction to the Massoretico-Critical Edition of the Hebrew Bible*, Trinitarian Bible Society, London, 1897.
Hertz, J H, *Daily Prayer Book*, Shapiro Vallentine and Co., London 1955.
Hertz, J H, *Pentateuch & Haftorahs*, Soncino Press, 2nd Ed., London, 1987.
Heschel, A J, *Heavenly Torah*, Continuum, NY, 2007.
Hirsch, S R, *The Pentateuch - translation and commentary*, Judaica Press, Gateshead, 1989.
Jastrow, M, *Dictionary of the Targumim, Talmud Babli, Yerushalmi and Midrashic Literature*, Judaic Press, New York, 1989.
Ed. Katz, S, *Hamaayan* #10:32, Internet, 1996.
Leiman, S, *Journal of Biblical Literature*, Sept. 1974.
Leibowitz, N, *Studies in Bamidbar*, World Zionist Organisation, Jerusalem, 1980.
Leitner, D, *Understanding the Alef-Beis*, Feldheim, Jerusalem, 2007.
Masechtot K'tanot - Sofrim, Sefer Torah, Avot d'Rabbi Natan, Ed. A. Cohen, Soncino Press Hebrew-English edition, 1984.
Milgrom, J, *The JPS Torah Commentary - Numbers*, JPS, Philadelphia/New York 1990.
Montefiore, C G & Loewe, H, A Rabbinic Anthology, Schocken Books, 1974.
Munk M, *The Wisdom of the Hebrew Alphabet*, Mesorah Publications, 1995.
Neusner, J, *Sifre to Numbers*, Vol. II, Scholars Press, Atlanta, 1986.
Pelcovitz, R, *Sforno - Commentary on the Torah*, Mesorah Publications, 1997.
Plaut, G, *The Torah - A Modern Commentary*, UAHC, New York, 1981.
Plaut, W G & Stern, C, *The Haftarah Commentary*, UAHC, New York, 1997.
Ed. Posner, R. & Ta-Shema, I, *The Hebrew Book - An Historical Survey*.
Rosenberg, D & Bloom, H, The Book of J, Faber and Faber 1990.
Silbermann, A, *Pentateuch with Rashi's Commentary, Bamidbar*, Jerusalem, 1933.

Soncino Talmud, Soncino Press Hebrew-English Edition - various dates.
Tov, E, *Textual Criticism of the Hebrew Bible, 3rd Ed.*, Fortress Press, 2012.
Yalkut Me'am Lo'ez on Bamidbar, Moznaim Publishing Corporation, 1990.

ABOUT THE AUTHOR

As well as being a marketing communications professional, Marc Michaels is also a practicing Jewish scribe *(Sofer STa"M)*. This involves writing, and restoration work on, sacred texts written on parchment with a feather quill.

Marc studied under the late Vivian Solomon *z'l* for five years and has an M.A. in Jewish studies from the Leo Baeck Rabbinical College.

His scribal website is at www.sofer.co.uk.

KULMUS PUBLISHING

Other books from Kulmus Publishing
(Print, pdf and epub versions all available through www.lulu.com and some through other on-line booksellers)

Megillat B'ney Chashmonay
(The Scroll of the Hasmonean Sons)
ISBN:978-0-9880539-0-8
Marc Michaels © 2013

There isn't a scroll read on *Chanukah* but perhaps there should be? *Sofer STa"M* Marc Michaels has gathered over twenty handwritten and printed manuscripts from the 13th Century onwards for this traditional text for *Chanukah* that used to be read in Italian, Yemenite and other synagogues.

Examining the variant Hebrew and Aramaic texts, he has created a new *tikkun kor'im* fully pointed with vowels and trope and a new *tikkun sofrim* with visual *midrashim* to add extra depth to the text. A new translation into English with explanatory notes is accompanied by a new commentary on the text - *Or LiM'norah* in the style of the biblical commentators. Includes two 'missing' verses found in the oldest Aramaic manuscripts but expunged from later Hebrew ones.

Tam (Simple)
ISBN978-0-9880539-7-7
Marc Michaels © 2017
PSALM 15 - KING DAVID'S GUIDE FOR THE SUCCESSFUL BUSINESS PERSON

King David has left us a person specification that we would be well served to adopt in today's business world where, sadly, ethics can be somewhat lacking.

In five short verses and a mere fifty-four words the character traits that are described, show those who engage in business the appropriate way to undertake that business. Marketer and scribe, Marc Michaels follows along David's Way to unlock the business lessons for today from Psalm 15.

Restoring the Tyburn Megillah
ISBN978-0-9810947-7-9
Marc Michaels © 2013

Jewish scribes don't often encounter Roman Catholic nuns. In a truly interfaith endeavour *Sofer STa"M* Mordechai Pinchas (Marc Michaels) chronicles the restoration of a several hundred year old manuscript of the book of Esther belonging to the nuns of the Tyburn Convent near Hyde Park.

Tikkun Megillat Hashoah
ISBN:978-0-9810947-1-7
Marc Michaels © 2008

Authorised by the Schechter Institute and the Rabbinic Assembly, this is the *Tikkun* (copyist's guide) for the *Megillat Hashoah* (Holocaust scroll). It contains the full unpointed text in full colour hand-written *STa"M*. It also supplies explanations of the various visual *midrashim* and information about how the scroll came to be written and the importance of this new piece of liturgy.

GIVE!
ISBN:978-0-9810947-6-2
Marc Michaels © 2009
An analysis of the biblical commandment to support the poor with particular reference to the Tannaitic interpretation in *Sifre* to *D'varim* 15:7-11. Discover how the ancient rabbis applied the *Torah* law to their own time and what lessons we might learn today about how best to ... GIVE! (169 pages with illustrations)

Megillat HaY'shuah
ISBN:978-0-9810947-9-3
Marc Michaels © 2008
The salvation scroll of the Yemenite Jews tells a parable of the dangers of the time to the Jewish population of Yemen and how Rabbi Shalom saves the day!

Sefer Binsoa
ISBN:978-0-9810947-7-9
Marc Michaels © 2010
In the majority of *Torah* scrolls *Bamidbar* l0:35-36 is encased between two critical marks, each taking the form of an inverted nun. *Sofer STa"M* Marc Michaels examines this unique visual midrash and provides a commentary that explains why *Sefer Binsoa* should be considered important and what lessons it might hold for us today.

Thoroughly Modern Moses
ISBN:978-0-9810947-4-8
Marc Michaels © 2009

Joseph Rosenberg, not so eminent Jewish scientist and time-traveller came to Earth with a bump and was surprised, nay shocked, to learn that he had landed on one of the most famous people in the history of history itself ... Moses the Lawgiver. Ordered to replace Moses by the Lord God Almighty, Supreme Being of the Universe and all round Nice-Guy, Mr. Rosenberg embarks on an adventure of biblical proportions. Will he survive? Will there be tea and cake? A science-fiction biblical comedy. Hitch-Hikers meets the Bible - enjoy! (Contains over 300 pages of laughter).

Shirat Ha-Olam - The Song of the World
ISBN: 978-0-9810947-0-0 Marc Michaels © 2009

Pictures from nature and around the world; words from the *Torah*, Prophets and Writings. Seventy digitally unaltered photographs matched to an appropriate biblical verse - each with its own story, told in this inspirational book. A feast for the eyes and the mind (149 pages set in a special *sofrut* inspired font and Palantino).

The Dot on the Ot
Marc Michaels © 2016

A tribute in the style of the wonderful 'Cat in the Hat', the 'Dot on the Ot' teaches about the famous dots on the letters that occur in the *Sefer Torah*. It has been created by Mordechai Pinchas HaSofer (aka Marc Michaels), *sofer STa"M* (scribe) for adults and children alike in loving memory of his wonderful nephew Nadav Ezra *z"l*. It is not intended for sale or profit. Download free from
http://www.sofer.co.uk/html/dots

The E-Fuzzy
ISBN:978-0-9810947-5-5
Marc Michaels © 2017

Too much screen time can be a bad thing for everyone! Will Popplethewaite ever understand why the children playing are so happy? Will the children rescue their Warm Fuzzy from his clutches? Or will they spend too much time staring at their E-Fuzzies to care? Find out in the 'The E-FUZZY'. A sequel to the excellent 'Original Warm Fuzzy Tale' by Claude M. Steiner. Written with kind permission of the original author. A cautionary TALE FOR EVERYONE. Illustrated throughout.

Mordy Potter and the Philosopher's Bagel
Marc Michaels © 2017

A Purim *shpiel* to delight young and old, very very loosely based on the Harry Potter books and films with a healthy dose of Jewish fun thrown in for good measure. With cast and props and stage directions, a ready made playlet written by *Sofer STa"M* Marc Michaels for you to adapt for your synagogue's Purim celebrations. A free download not for sale from Kulmus Publishing. Download link: bit.ly/2kMsvzG

Welcome to the Cavalcade
A *Festschrift* in honour of
Rabbi Professor Jonathan Magonet
Edited by Rabbi Howard Cooper, Rabbi Colin Eimer
and Rabbi Elli Tikvah Sarah
Various Contributors © 2013
A celebration by his rabbinic and academic colleagues of Rabbi Professor Jonathan Magonet's unique contribution to the Jewish and wider world.

Festschrift for
Rabbi Maurice Michaels
ISBN:978-0-9810947-8-6
Edited by Marc Michaels © 2011
A collection of essays on Jewish themes to mark the occasion of Rabbi Maurice Michaels' 70th birthday written by many of his rabbinical colleagues.

Tales from the Rabbi's Desk Vol. 1
ISBN:978-0-9880539-2-2
Rabbi Walter Rothschild © 2015
Rabbi Walter Rothschild brings us a collection of stories, some fiction, some based on fact that give an insight into the rich tapestry of human lives that he and his colleagues have touched.

Tales from the Rabbi's Desk Vol. 2
ISBN:978-0-9880539-5-3
Rabbi Walter Rothschild © 2016
Rabbi Walter Rothschild presents a second selection of his 'Tales', based on his own experience and those of his colleagues, all working at that invisible interface between the Human and the Divine.

Women Rabbis in the Pulpit
ISBN:978-0-9880539-3-9
Editors: Rabbi Dr Barbara Borts & Rabbi Elli Tikvah Sarah © 2015

A collection of sermons by women rabbis dedicated to the memory of the first woman Rabbi, Regina Jonas who was ordained on December 27, 1935. Sermons cover topics under the headings Living a Jewish Life, Being Human, God and Spirituality, Responses and Responsibility to the World, Feminism and Gender and Life and Loss.

Care of Your Torah - A Guide
ISBN:978-0-9810947-2-4
Marc Michaels © 2008

A short 19 page guide written by a *Sofer STa"M* (scribe) to help Synagogues care for their Torah scrolls. With lots of useful tips and photographs showing many examples of what can make a Torah *pasul* (not kosher).

The East London Synagogue - Outpost of another World
ISBN:978-0-9810947-3-1
Marc Michaels © 2008

A short history of the early days of the East London Synagogue, Rectory Square, and an examination of how it came to be established in 1877. Described by the Revd. Joseph Stern as 'a rallying point in this locality' what was the intended role for this 'outpost of another world'? Did it succeed? An examination of the historical documents together with rare photos taken shortly before the closure of the building, and from other sources.

www.ingramcontent.com/pod-product-compliance
Lightning Source LLC
Chambersburg PA
CBHW032022040426
42448CB00006B/707